The Shadow Key

The Shadow Key

Matthew Petchinsky

1

The Shadow Key: Unlocking the Power of Your Dark Self
By: Matthew Petchinsky

Disclaimer

This book is a work of personal development, psychological exploration, and symbolic interpretation. *The Shadow Key: Unlocking the Power of Your Dark Self* is not intended to replace, substitute, or override professional medical, psychological, psychiatric, legal, or spiritual care. The concepts, frameworks, metaphors, and practices described within are offered for educational and reflective purposes only.

Any references to the "dark self," "shadow," "inner power," or "unlocking" are symbolic and introspective in nature. They are not instructions to engage in harmful behavior toward oneself or others, nor do they encourage self-destructive, antisocial, illegal, or violent actions. This book does not promote nihilism, cruelty, domination, or the rejection of personal responsibility. Instead, it explores the often-ignored aspects of identity—such as fear, anger, grief, desire, and suppressed instinct—as psychological material that can be acknowledged, understood, and integrated in a healthy and ethical way.

Readers are responsible for their own interpretations and actions. Emotional responses may arise while engaging with this material, particularly for those with past trauma, unresolved grief, anxiety, depression, or other mental health conditions. If at any point the content feels overwhelming, destabilizing, or distressing, the reader is strongly encouraged to pause and seek guidance from a qualified mental health professional. This book is not designed as a crisis intervention tool.

Nothing in this work should be construed as a diagnosis, treatment plan, or therapeutic directive. Individual experiences will vary, and results are neither guaranteed nor promised. Growth, insight, and empowerment require personal agency, self-reflection, and ethical discernment.

This book does not align itself with or promote any organized religion, ideology, or belief system. References to darkness, shadow, or power are used in a psychological, archetypal, and symbolic sense rather than a literal, supernatural, or dogmatic one.

By choosing to read *The Shadow Key*, the reader acknowledges that they are engaging with material that invites introspection and personal responsibility. The author assumes no liability for how this content is interpreted, applied, or misapplied.

Proceed with self-awareness, grounded judgment, and respect for both yourself and others.

Introduction

Most people spend their lives trying to become "better" by cutting parts of themselves away.

They silence their anger.
They bury their grief.
They deny their hunger for control, recognition, or intensity.
They label certain thoughts as unacceptable, certain feelings as shameful, certain instincts as dangerous.

And then they wonder why they feel hollow.

The Shadow Key begins with a different premise:
What if the parts of you that were rejected were never the problem?
What if they were the source of your strength—misunderstood, unmanaged, but powerful?

The "dark self" is not evil. It is not broken. It is not something to be exorcised, conquered, or erased. It is the collection of traits, impulses, emotions, and truths that were pushed out of sight because they made others uncomfortable—or because you were taught that survival required silence.

The shadow forms early. It grows every time you learn that being fully honest costs you love, safety, or belonging. It grows when you're praised for being agreeable instead of authentic. It grows when pain has nowhere to go but inward.

And yet—nothing in the human psyche disappears just because it's ignored.

What is denied becomes distorted.
What is suppressed becomes explosive.
What is unlived seeks expression in other ways.

This book is not about indulging darkness.
It is about *unlocking it*—with intention, discipline, and responsibility.

Because power does not come from pretending you are light alone. It comes from knowing exactly what you are capable of—and choosing consciously.

The shadow contains anger, yes—but also boundaries.
It contains desire—but also ambition.
It contains fear—but also instinct, intuition, and clarity.

Many people fear their dark self because they were never taught how to hold it. They were only taught how to repress it. Society rewards restraint without teaching integration. Control without comprehension. Obedience without self-knowledge.

But repression is not the same as mastery.

Mastery begins with awareness.

This book offers no fantasy of instant transformation, no promise of becoming untouchable or dominant overnight. Instead, it provides a framework for understanding how the shadow operates, why it exists, and how it can be turned from an unconscious force into a conscious ally.

You will not be asked to destroy parts of yourself.
You will be asked to meet them honestly.

That meeting can be uncomfortable. Sometimes painful. Often illuminating.

Because the shadow holds not only what you fear—but what you were never allowed to become.

Within it live the assertive words you swallowed.
The instincts you second-guessed.
The anger that tried to protect you before it was labeled "too much."
The ambition you were told to tone down.
The hunger to take up space.

This book treats those elements not as flaws to be corrected, but as signals to be decoded.

You are not broken for having a shadow.
You are human.

What determines whether the shadow harms or strengthens you is not its existence—but your relationship to it.

Ignored, it sabotages.
Feared, it leaks sideways.
Integrated, it becomes precision.

Throughout these pages, you will be invited to slow down, reflect, and observe yourself without moral panic. You will be encouraged to replace judgment with curiosity, and fear with discernment. This is not about becoming ruthless or detached—it is about becoming *whole*.

Wholeness is not softness alone.
It is stability under pressure.
It is clarity in moments of emotional charge.
It is knowing when to yield and when to stand firm.

The shadow does not erase compassion—it sharpens it.
It does not cancel morality—it grounds it in reality.

Many people who avoid their shadow believe they are being virtuous. In truth, they are often being fragile—because they have never tested their inner strength.

This book does not glorify darkness. It respects it.

There is a difference.

You will not be told what to feel or who to become. You will be given language, structure, and insight so that you can understand yourself more clearly—and act with greater intention.

The key you are being offered is not external.
It has always been yours.

But keys require readiness. They open doors that cannot be unopened.

That is why this work asks for honesty above comfort, responsibility above fantasy, and self-awareness above performance.

If you are looking for validation without reflection, this book will challenge you.
If you are looking for power without accountability, this book will frustrate you.

If you are willing to meet yourself without flinching, this book will serve you.

The shadow is not your enemy.

It is the part of you that remembers who you were before you learned to disappear.

And the key has been waiting.

Chapter 1: What Is the Shadow Self?

The Part of You That Was Not Allowed to Exist

The shadow self is not something you were born fearing. It became hidden because it was *unwelcome*. From an early age, you learned which emotions earned approval and which ones cost you connection. Anger was called disrespect. Curiosity became disobedience. Desire was labeled inappropriate. Instinct was framed as danger. Slowly, the parts of you that threatened harmony or control were pushed out of view.

This process is rarely intentional or cruel. Parents, teachers, cultures, and systems pass down survival rules they themselves inherited. They teach restraint before understanding, obedience before self-knowledge. The shadow forms not because you are flawed, but because you adapted. You learned which parts of yourself were "too much" for the environments you depended on.

What goes unexpressed does not dissolve. It waits. The shadow becomes a storage place for unfinished emotions, unspoken truths, and unrealized potential. It carries the anger you swallowed, the confidence you muted, the boundaries you never set. Over time, it gathers weight—not as corruption, but as pressure.

Many people mistake the shadow for negativity or moral failure. In reality, it is neutral energy shaped by context. The same anger that protects a boundary can become resentment when ignored. The same ambition that drives growth can become sabotage when denied. The shadow is not inherently destructive—it becomes so only when left unconscious.

To understand the shadow is to understand the cost of adaptation. Every trait hidden once helped you survive. This chapter begins by removing shame from that truth. You did not choose your shadow. You inherited it through experience.

How Suppression Becomes Power Without Direction

Suppression is often praised as maturity. You're told to "be the bigger person," "let it go," or "stay calm." But calm without honesty is not balance—it is containment. When emotions are suppressed instead of processed, they do not disappear. They turn inward, looking for expression through indirect routes.

This is why suppressed anger becomes passive aggression. Why unacknowledged grief turns into numbness. Why denied desire shows up as obsession or avoidance. The shadow leaks through behavior when it is not allowed language. It seeks outlets when it is denied acknowledgment.

Power lives inside these suppressed traits. Anger contains clarity. Fear contains instinct. Desire contains direction. When these forces are cut off from conscious awareness, they operate without guidance. The shadow does not disappear—it becomes autonomous.

This autonomy is what people fear. They say, "I don't want to lose control," without realizing that suppression *is* the loss of control. What you refuse to face will act through you rather than with you. The shadow takes the wheel when the conscious self pretends it isn't there.

Understanding the shadow means reclaiming authorship. It means turning raw emotional energy into something usable instead of reactive. The goal is not indulgence, but direction. Not expression without restraint, but awareness with choice.

Power is not dangerous when it is seen. It becomes dangerous only when it is denied.

The Shadow Is Not Evil—It Is Unintegrated

The word "dark" has been burdened with moral judgment. Darkness is equated with harm, corruption, or malice. But psychologically, darkness simply means *unseen*. The shadow is what exists outside conscious identity—not what exists outside morality.

Many traits placed in the shadow are socially inconvenient, not ethically wrong. Assertiveness becomes labeled selfish. Confidence becomes arrogance. Sensitivity becomes weakness. The shadow often contains traits that were too strong, not too cruel.

When people fear their shadow, they are often fearing their own capacity. They worry that acknowledging anger will make them violent, or that recognizing desire will make them reckless. This fear misunderstands integration. Awareness does not amplify impulses—it refines them.

Integration means allowing traits to exist in consciousness where they can be evaluated, guided, and balanced. The shadow becomes dangerous only when it is denied entry into awareness. Light does not erase darkness; it reveals shape and boundary.

To call the shadow evil is to misunderstand its origin. It formed to protect you. It adapted to constraints. It learned silence where expression was unsafe. It carries intelligence born of experience, not corruption.

When you stop moralizing the shadow, you can begin listening to it.

Where the Shadow Shows Up in Daily Life

The shadow announces itself quietly. It appears in overreactions that surprise you. In jealousy that feels disproportionate. In irritation that lingers longer than it should. These moments are not failures—they are messages.

Pay attention to what irritates you in others. Often, the traits that provoke strong reactions mirror something you disowned in yourself. Judgment becomes a projection screen for the shadow. What you condemn externally may be what you fear internally.

The shadow also appears in patterns. Repeating conflicts. Self-sabotage near success. Attraction to situations that replicate old wounds. These are not accidents. They are attempts at resolution—unfinished emotional business seeking closure.

Avoidance is another signal. The topics you refuse to think about, the conversations you delay, the decisions you postpone. The shadow often guards thresholds you are not ready to cross—but readiness grows through acknowledgment.

When you observe these patterns without shame, the shadow stops shouting. It begins communicating.

The Difference Between Shadow and Trauma

Not all pain belongs to the shadow, and not all shadow work is trauma work. Trauma involves overwhelming experiences that disrupted your sense of safety. The shadow includes traits, impulses, and emotions that were suppressed—sometimes because of trauma, sometimes because of social conditioning.

Confusing the two can be harmful. The shadow is not something to "heal" away. It is something to *integrate*. Trauma requires care, pacing, and often professional support. Shadow work requires honesty, reflection, and responsibility.

Some parts of the shadow formed to protect you during difficult periods. Others formed simply because the environment did not allow complexity. Not every hidden trait is wounded—some are simply unused.

Understanding this distinction prevents turning shadow work into self-pathologizing. You are not broken for having a shadow. You are layered. The goal is not excavation without care, but integration with discernment.

Approach the shadow as a relationship, not a battlefield.

Integration: Turning the Shadow Into an Ally

Integration does not mean acting on every impulse. It means understanding what each impulse wants and deciding how to respond consciously. The shadow does not demand obedience—it asks for recognition.

When integrated, anger becomes boundary-setting. Fear becomes intuition. Desire becomes direction. The shadow stops undermining and starts informing. It becomes a source of clarity rather than chaos.

This process requires maturity. Integration asks you to hold opposing truths without collapsing into extremes. You can be compassionate and firm. Controlled and expressive. Powerful and ethical.

The shadow is not meant to dominate your identity. It is meant to complete it. Wholeness is not purity—it is balance informed by awareness.

Integration is not a destination. It is a practice.

Dark Self's Advice

You keep pretending I am the problem, but I was born from your silence. I carry what you were not allowed to say, feel, or become. I do not want to ruin you—I want to be acknowledged. When you ignore me, I push. When you listen, I guide.

I am not asking you to lose control. I am asking you to stop lying to yourself. I already know what you feel. I already know what you want. The only question is whether you will meet me consciously—or let me speak through reaction.

Exercises

Exercise 1: Shadow Mapping

1. Write down three traits you were discouraged from expressing as a child.
2. Note when each trait shows up indirectly in your adult life.
3. Identify one healthy way each trait could be expressed consciously.

Exercise 2: Trigger Tracking

1. For one week, note moments of strong emotional reaction.
2. Identify the emotion beneath the reaction.
3. Ask what boundary, desire, or fear is being signaled.

Exercise 3: Trait Reclamation

1. Choose one shadow trait you avoid.
2. Write how it once protected you.
3. Define one responsible way to allow it expression now.

Journal Prompts

1. What emotion do I judge myself for most?
2. When do I feel "too much"?
3. What do I envy in others?
4. What reaction embarrasses me afterward?
5. What truth do I avoid admitting?
6. When do I feel most constrained?
7. What do I fear would happen if I were fully honest?
8. What part of me feels misunderstood?
9. When do I feel most powerful—and why?
10. What am I afraid to want?

Closing Reflection

The shadow is not a threat to your integrity—it is a test of your honesty. What you bring into awareness loses the power to control you from the dark. This chapter is not an invitation to act impulsively, but to see clearly. Integration begins not with change, but with recognition. The key is not force. It is truth.

Chapter 2: Confronting the Hidden Aspects of Your Mind

The Mind's Unlit Corridors

Your mind is not a single, unified voice. It is a layered structure built over years of experience, adaptation, and memory. Some thoughts are allowed to speak freely. Others are redirected, softened, or silenced altogether. The hidden aspects of your mind are not random—they exist because certain truths were inconvenient, unsafe, or disruptive at the time they emerged.

These unlit corridors form when awareness is narrowed for survival. When situations demand composure, silence, or compliance, the mind learns to reroute intensity elsewhere. Thoughts do not disappear simply because they are unwelcome. They retreat into quieter spaces, waiting for conditions where they can surface without penalty.

Confronting these hidden aspects requires slowing down. The conscious mind prefers speed and certainty. It wants clarity without complexity. The hidden mind operates differently. It communicates through patterns, discomfort, and repetition. You encounter it when something feels familiar but unresolved.

Avoidance keeps these corridors dark. Busyness, distraction, and constant stimulation act as barriers against introspection. Many people fear stillness because stillness allows unfiltered thoughts to rise. But the discomfort you fear is not harm—it is information.

To confront the hidden mind is to choose awareness over avoidance. This choice does not demand aggression or force. It demands patience, curiosity, and the willingness to stay present with what arises.

Why Certain Thoughts Are Buried

Thoughts are buried because they challenge identity. The mind protects coherence, even at the cost of truth. When a thought threatens how you see yourself—or how others see you—it is often pushed aside. This is not weakness; it is preservation.

Shame is one of the strongest forces behind mental concealment. When a thought carries emotional risk—fear of rejection, punishment, or loss—it is flagged as dangerous. The mind responds by minimizing or rationalizing it away.

Over time, this creates blind spots. You may believe you are calm when you are resentful, generous when you are depleted, patient when you are afraid of conflict. These distortions are not lies—they are compromises.

Hidden thoughts often resurface under pressure. Stress, fatigue, or emotional vulnerability lower the mind's defenses. This is why certain truths emerge during conflict or exhaustion. The buried mind waits for openings.

Confrontation does not mean indulging every thought. It means acknowledging its existence without immediate judgment. Awareness is the first act of control.

Resistance as a Signal, Not an Obstacle

Resistance is often mistaken for failure. When discomfort arises, many people retreat, assuming they are doing something wrong. In reality, resistance is a signal that you are approaching material that matters.

The mind resists change because change requires reorganization. Old beliefs, habits, and identities must loosen to make room for new understanding. Resistance protects stability, even when that stability is limiting.

When confronting hidden aspects of the mind, resistance may show up as distraction, irritation, self-doubt, or sudden fatigue. These reactions are not signs to stop—they are signs to slow down and observe.

Treat resistance as communication. Ask what it is guarding. Often, beneath resistance is fear of loss—loss of identity, certainty, or control. Acknowledging this fear reduces its intensity.

Confrontation becomes safer when you approach resistance with respect instead of force. The goal is understanding, not conquest.

The Role of Self-Deception

Self-deception is not dishonesty—it is adaptation. The mind tells stories to maintain continuity and self-worth. These stories may omit, soften, or reframe certain truths. Over time, they become familiar narratives that feel real.

Confronting hidden aspects requires questioning these narratives. This can be unsettling. When a story collapses, it leaves uncertainty behind. The mind resists this gap, preferring a flawed certainty over an unknown truth.

Self-deception often hides emotional needs. A belief like "I don't care" may mask disappointment. "I'm fine alone" may conceal loneliness. These statements are not false—they are incomplete.

The danger of self-deception lies not in its existence, but in its permanence. When stories go unexamined, they limit growth. Confrontation invites revision, not condemnation.

You are not betraying yourself by questioning your narratives. You are refining them.

Facing Discomfort Without Collapse

Discomfort is the gateway to awareness, but it must be approached with structure. Uncontained introspection can overwhelm. The goal is to face discomfort without drowning in it.

Grounding practices—breath, body awareness, pacing—keep confrontation manageable. You do not need to uncover everything at once. The mind reveals what you are ready to hold.

When difficult thoughts arise, notice their physical impact. Tension, heat, or constriction often accompany hidden material. These sensations are signals, not threats. Staying present allows them to pass.

Avoid moralizing your thoughts. A thought is not an action. Allowing awareness does not mean endorsement. This distinction preserves safety while encouraging honesty.

Facing discomfort builds resilience. Each time you stay present, the hidden mind learns that awareness is not dangerous.

Clarity as the Outcome of Confrontation

Confrontation is not about tearing yourself apart. It is about bringing fragmented awareness into coherence. Clarity emerges when hidden aspects are acknowledged and contextualized.

When the mind is no longer divided against itself, energy is freed. Less effort is spent suppressing, justifying, or avoiding. Decisions become simpler because they are informed by fuller understanding.

Clarity does not eliminate complexity. It allows you to hold complexity without confusion. You can recognize conflicting desires without being paralyzed by them.

This clarity supports agency. When you understand your motives, fears, and patterns, you act with intention rather than impulse. The shadow becomes a source of insight rather than disruption.

Confrontation is not an end—it is a foundation for conscious choice.

Dark Self's Advice

You don't need to force your way into the hidden parts of your mind. I reveal myself when you stop pretending you already know everything about yourself. The moment you allow uncertainty, the door opens.

Stop asking whether a thought is acceptable and start asking what it is trying to tell you. I don't speak in absolutes. I speak in signals. Learn the language instead of silencing the message.

Exercises

Exercise 1: Thought Inventory

1. Sit quietly for ten minutes and write down every thought that arises without filtering.
2. Highlight the thoughts you feel tempted to justify or dismiss.
3. Reflect on what emotion each highlighted thought carries.

Exercise 2: Resistance Dialogue

1. Identify a topic you avoid thinking about.
2. Write a dialogue between yourself and the resistance you feel.
3. Ask what it is protecting and why.

Exercise 3: Narrative Deconstruction

1. Write a belief you hold strongly about yourself.
2. List evidence that supports it and evidence that challenges it.
3. Rewrite the belief in a more nuanced form.

Journal Prompts

1. What thoughts do I immediately judge?
2. When do I distract myself from reflection?
3. What belief feels fragile?
4. What discomfort do I avoid most?
5. When do I feel mentally divided?
6. What truth feels dangerous to admit?
7. What emotion do I minimize?
8. When do my actions contradict my words?
9. What story do I repeat about myself?
10. What am I afraid clarity would require me to change?

Closing Reflection

Confronting the hidden aspects of your mind is an act of courage, not aggression. Each moment of awareness restores integrity. You are not dismantling yourself—you are reclaiming coherence. The mind does not resist truth; it resists unprepared exposure. With patience and structure, clarity becomes a steady companion rather than a sudden shock.

Chapter 3: Transforming Fear into Power

Fear as a Signal, Not a Sentence

Fear is often treated as an endpoint—a stop sign that signals danger, failure, or incapacity. From an early age, you may have learned to interpret fear as weakness or warning alone. But fear is not a verdict. It is information. It is the nervous system's way of drawing attention to something that matters.

Every fear points to a threshold. It arises at the edge of uncertainty, growth, or potential loss. If fear were only a signal of danger, it would be simpler. But fear also appears when you are close to something meaningful—change, visibility, intimacy, or power. This is why fear often intensifies before expansion.

When fear is misunderstood, it becomes paralyzing. You avoid decisions, delay action, and shrink possibilities to maintain comfort. Over time, fear hardens into limitation. What began as a momentary signal becomes a governing force.

Transforming fear begins by changing how you listen to it. Instead of asking, "What could go wrong?" you ask, "What is this fear protecting?" Often, the answer reveals a value—safety, belonging, competence—that deserves attention, not avoidance.

Fear does not demand obedience. It asks for interpretation.

The Origins of Fear Conditioning

Fear is shaped by experience. Some fears are instinctive, rooted in survival. Others are learned through repetition, punishment, or observation. When a situation once caused pain, embarrassment, or rejection, the mind marks similar situations as threats.

This conditioning can persist long after the original danger has passed. The body reacts before the mind has time to evaluate. Heart rate increases, muscles tense, and avoidance impulses activate. This reaction feels immediate and convincing.

Understanding the origin of a fear reduces its authority. When you identify where a fear was learned, you can separate past conditions from present reality. The fear may still arise, but it no longer dictates behavior automatically.

Conditioned fear often guards outdated identities. You may fear speaking up because silence once ensured safety. You may fear success because visibility once attracted scrutiny. These fears were adaptive—but adaptation does not require permanence.

Power emerges when you update the fear's role from commander to advisor.

Fear and the Shadow's Energy

Fear is closely linked to the shadow because it often guards suppressed desires and strengths. What you fear confronting may be what you fear *becoming*. Assertiveness, leadership, independence—these traits can feel dangerous if they conflict with how you learned to belong.

The shadow holds not only what you avoid, but what you are capable of. Fear acts as a gatekeeper, testing readiness. When fear arises around a potential action, it may indicate proximity to latent power.

This is why fear and excitement often feel similar in the body. Both involve heightened arousal and uncertainty. The difference lies in interpretation. When fear is framed as threat, you retreat. When framed as activation, you advance with caution.

Transforming fear does not mean eliminating it. It means redirecting its energy. Fear sharpens focus, heightens awareness, and mobilizes resources. When consciously engaged, it becomes fuel.

The shadow does not want fear removed. It wants fear *used*.

Choosing Response Over Reaction

Reaction is automatic. Response is deliberate. Fear pushes toward reaction—freeze, flee, or appease. Transformation begins when you insert choice between sensation and action.

This pause does not need to be long. Even a moment of breath can shift control from reflex to awareness. In that moment, you acknowledge the fear without submitting to it.

Choosing response requires self-trust. You trust that you can tolerate discomfort long enough to decide. This trust grows through practice, not perfection. Each time you respond consciously, fear's grip loosens slightly.

Over time, fear learns that awareness does not equal danger. The nervous system recalibrates. Situations that once triggered avoidance become manageable.

Power is not fearlessness. It is steadiness in the presence of fear.

Reclaiming Agency Through Exposure

Avoidance strengthens fear. Exposure—intentional, paced engagement—weakens it. This does not mean throwing yourself into overwhelming situations. It means meeting fear incrementally, with awareness and support.

When you approach what you fear in manageable steps, you gather evidence of competence. Each successful engagement updates the mind's threat assessment. Fear loses credibility as an absolute authority.

Exposure also reveals false assumptions. You learn that discomfort is tolerable, that outcomes are rarely catastrophic, and that recovery is possible. These realizations transform fear from a barrier into a challenge.

Agency grows when you act despite fear, not in its absence. Each action reinforces the belief that you are capable of navigating uncertainty.

Fear becomes a training ground for resilience.

Power Defined by Self-Trust

True power is internal. It is the confidence that you can meet difficulty without abandoning yourself. This confidence is built through repeated acts of conscious engagement with fear.

As fear transforms, it no longer dictates boundaries. It highlights areas for growth. You begin to recognize fear as a companion rather than an enemy—a signal that you are alive, invested, and stretching.

Self-trust replaces self-protection. You still assess risk, but you do not retreat from possibility by default. You choose alignment over avoidance.

Power does not eliminate vulnerability. It integrates it. You move forward with awareness, not bravado.

Fear, once transformed, becomes momentum.

Dark Self's Advice

I don't want you fearless. I want you *awake*. Fear sharpens you when you stop running from it. I rise when you choose to stay present instead of disappearing.

Stop asking me to calm down. Ask me what I'm preparing you for. I don't block your power—I announce it.

Exercises

Exercise 1: Fear Deconstruction

1. Write down a current fear.
2. Identify what outcome you are trying to avoid.
3. List what value or need this fear is protecting.
4. Decide one small action that honors the value without avoiding the situation.

Exercise 2: Response Practice

1. Notice a moment of fear during the day.
2. Pause and take three slow breaths.
3. Choose one deliberate action instead of the automatic reaction.
4. Reflect on the outcome.

Exercise 3: Incremental Exposure

1. Identify a fear-based avoidance pattern.
2. Break the feared situation into three manageable steps.
3. Engage with the first step consciously.
4. Record sensations, thoughts, and results after each attempt.

Journal Prompts

1. What fear shows up repeatedly?
2. What do I believe fear says about me?
3. When has fear kept me safe?
4. When has fear limited me?
5. What power might fear be guarding?
6. How do I usually react to fear?
7. What would response look like instead?
8. What discomfort am I capable of tolerating?
9. What evidence contradicts my fear?
10. Who might I become if fear informed rather than controlled me?

Closing Reflection

Fear is not a flaw in your design—it is part of your guidance system. When you meet fear with awareness instead of avoidance, it shifts from obstruction to orientation. Power grows where fear is understood, not eliminated. This chapter invites you to stop negotiating your life around fear and start using it as a compass toward conscious strength.

Chapter 4: The Role of the Subconscious in Shadow Work

The Subconscious as the Keeper of What You Forgot

The subconscious mind is not passive storage. It is an active curator of experience, continuously sorting, categorizing, and protecting information that the conscious mind cannot or will not hold. Every moment you dismissed, suppressed, or rushed past left a trace. The subconscious remembers what the conscious self chose to forget.

Unlike conscious thought, the subconscious does not operate in linear time. Past experiences remain present, influencing perception and behavior long after the original event has ended. This is why certain reactions feel immediate and disproportionate—the subconscious is responding to accumulated memory, not the current moment alone.

Shadow work depends on understanding this dynamic. The shadow does not originate in logic or reasoning; it originates in unprocessed experience stored below awareness. The subconscious acts as the bridge between lived history and present behavior.

When the subconscious senses threat, it activates patterns automatically. These patterns may no longer be relevant, but they persist because they once ensured safety. Without awareness, the shadow expresses itself through these automatic responses.

To work with the shadow is to learn the language of the subconscious—symbolic, emotional, and pattern-based rather than verbal or rational.

Why the Subconscious Speaks in Symbols

The subconscious does not communicate in sentences. It communicates through images, sensations, emotions, dreams, and repetition. These symbols condense complex experience into manageable signals. What cannot be spoken directly is translated into metaphor.

This is why shadow material often surfaces indirectly. You may feel unease without knowing why, dream of places you have never been, or react strongly to seemingly minor events. These are not random—they are symbolic expressions seeking interpretation.

The conscious mind prefers clarity and explanation. The subconscious prefers resonance. When something "hits a nerve," it is because the subconscious recognizes a pattern that the conscious mind has not yet named.

Ignoring these signals deepens disconnection. Interpreting them with curiosity opens communication. Shadow work is less about decoding meaning immediately and more about noticing what repeats.

Symbols lose their power when they are acknowledged. What once haunted becomes informative.

How Conditioning Lives Below Awareness

Conditioning is stored in the subconscious as associations. Experiences are linked with emotions, outcomes, and expectations. Over time, these links form predictive models that guide behavior automatically.

If vulnerability once led to pain, the subconscious associates openness with danger. If visibility once attracted criticism, the subconscious equates success with threat. These associations persist even when circumstances change.

The conscious mind may disagree, but the subconscious prioritizes safety over accuracy. It reacts faster than logic because it evolved to protect. This is why insight alone does not dissolve patterns—experience must update the subconscious.

Shadow work engages these layers by bringing awareness to conditioned responses. When you notice a pattern without judgment, you create space for change. Awareness interrupts automaticity.

The subconscious learns through repetition and emotional safety. Each conscious response teaches it that the present is different from the past.

Dreams, Imagination, and the Shadow

Dreams are one of the subconscious's most direct communication channels. During sleep, the conscious mind relaxes its control, allowing symbolic material to surface. Dreams often reveal what the waking mind avoids.

Imagination functions similarly. When you allow mental images without censorship, the subconscious expresses itself creatively. This is why guided imagery and visualization can access shadow material gently.

Shadow work does not require literal interpretation of dreams or images. Their emotional tone matters more than their narrative. How a dream feels often reveals more than what happens.

Keeping a record of dreams, symbols, and recurring imagery builds fluency. Over time, patterns emerge that illuminate subconscious concerns and desires.

The goal is not to analyze obsessively, but to listen attentively.

Reprogramming Through Conscious Engagement

The subconscious cannot be argued with—it must be shown. Reprogramming occurs through experience, repetition, and emotional congruence. When conscious action aligns with awareness, the subconscious updates its expectations.

Shadow work creates new associations. When you face discomfort safely, the subconscious learns that awareness is not dangerous. When you express a boundary and survive, it learns that assertion does not equal loss.

Consistency matters more than intensity. Small, repeated acts of conscious engagement reshape subconscious patterns gradually.

This process requires patience. The subconscious changes through trust built over time. Force creates resistance; curiosity invites cooperation.

Integration occurs when conscious and subconscious goals align.

The Subconscious as an Ally, Not an Obstacle

Many people treat the subconscious as a saboteur. In reality, it is loyal—to outdated instructions. It does not oppose growth; it protects survival strategies learned under previous conditions.

When you respect this role, cooperation becomes possible. You stop fighting yourself and start updating internal agreements. Shadow work becomes dialogue rather than domination.

The subconscious responds to compassion and clarity. When it feels acknowledged, it relaxes its grip. Patterns soften. Reactivity decreases.

Your shadow is not hidden because it is malicious. It is hidden because it was stored for later. Shadow work is the act of retrieval.

The subconscious does not need to be conquered—it needs to be understood.

Dark Self's Advice

You keep trying to reason your way past me, but I don't live in logic. I live in memory, sensation, and symbol. If you want to work with me, slow down enough to feel.

Stop demanding instant clarity. I reveal myself when you create safety. Show me through your actions that awareness will not destroy you, and I will stop hiding.

Exercises

Exercise 1: Pattern Recognition

1. Identify a recurring emotional reaction.
2. Trace it back to the earliest memory you can recall.
3. Note the belief or expectation formed.
4. Write how this pattern shows up today.

Exercise 2: Symbol Journaling

1. Write down any recurring dreams, images, or metaphors.
2. Describe the emotions associated with each.
3. Reflect on where these emotions appear in waking life.

Exercise 3: Subconscious Reassurance

1. Choose a feared or avoided action.
2. Engage with it in a safe, manageable way.
3. Afterward, write a reassurance statement to your subconscious describing the outcome.

Journal Prompts

1. What reactions feel automatic?
2. What symbols appear repeatedly in my thoughts or dreams?
3. When do I feel a response before I understand it?
4. What patterns frustrate me most?
5. What does my subconscious prioritize?
6. What experiences shaped this priority?
7. Where do I feel tension without clear cause?
8. What does safety mean to me?
9. What belief no longer fits my life?
10. How can I show my subconscious that the present is different?

Closing Reflection

The subconscious is not separate from you—it is a deeper layer of you. Shadow work becomes sustainable when you stop forcing insight and start building trust. Awareness teaches the subconscious that it no longer has to protect you alone. Integration happens when memory, meaning, and choice move in the same direction.

Chapter 5: Healing Through Darkness

Why Healing Does Not Begin in the Light

Healing is often imagined as a movement toward positivity, peace, and relief. While those qualities may emerge over time, they are rarely the starting point. Healing begins where discomfort is acknowledged rather than avoided. It begins in the places where pain was stored because it could not be expressed safely.

Darkness, in this context, is not despair or destruction. It is the territory of honesty. It is where grief, anger, shame, and fear were placed when there was no space for them elsewhere. Healing through darkness means entering these territories with awareness and intention.

Many people try to heal by bypassing what hurts. They seek affirmation without examination, calm without confrontation. This approach offers temporary relief but leaves core wounds untouched. The darkness persists, unseen and unresolved.

When you allow yourself to meet what was hidden, the nervous system begins to release its grip. Pain loses its intensity when it is witnessed without judgment. Darkness softens when it is approached with care.

Healing does not require you to relive every wound. It requires you to stop abandoning yourself at the point of discomfort.

The Difference Between Processing and Reopening Wounds

There is a critical distinction between healing and re-injury. Healing through darkness is not about retraumatization. It is about processing experiences that were never fully integrated.

Reopening a wound involves reliving it without support or structure. Processing involves acknowledging the emotional residue while remaining anchored in the present. Shadow work emphasizes processing, not immersion.

The body plays a key role in this distinction. When healing is occurring, sensations may arise but remain manageable. When re-injury occurs, overwhelm takes over. Learning to notice this difference protects your well-being.

Healing requires pacing. You do not need to confront everything at once. The subconscious reveals what you are ready to handle. Respecting this rhythm prevents collapse.

Darkness heals when it is met with containment, not force.

Compassion for the Parts That Survived

Many shadow aspects formed to protect you during difficult periods. Anger defended boundaries when words failed. Numbness reduced pain when feeling was too costly. Withdrawal preserved safety when connection felt dangerous.

Healing through darkness involves recognizing these strategies with gratitude rather than shame. You survived because of them. They were solutions under constrained conditions.

Compassion transforms how these parts respond. When you stop condemning them, they no longer need to cling to outdated roles. They relax when they feel acknowledged.

This compassion extends to your past self. You made choices with the resources available at the time. Healing is not rewriting history—it is understanding it.

Darkness becomes less threatening when it is recognized as resilience rather than failure.

Integrating Pain Without Letting It Define You

Pain is informative, but it is not identity. Healing through darkness requires holding pain without letting it dominate self-concept. You can honor suffering without becoming consumed by it.

Integration means allowing pain to exist alongside other experiences. Joy, strength, and clarity can coexist with unresolved areas. Healing is not linear; it is layered.

When pain is denied, it seeks attention. When it is acknowledged, it settles. Integration reduces its urgency. You gain choice in how you respond.

This balance requires boundaries. You engage with pain intentionally rather than constantly. You create time-limited spaces for reflection, then return to daily life.

Healing becomes sustainable when pain is part of the whole, not the whole story.

Darkness as a Source of Wisdom

Pain carries information about needs, values, and limits. Darkness reveals where care was missing, where boundaries were crossed, and where authenticity was sacrificed.

When you listen to this information, healing becomes instructive rather than punitive. You learn what to protect, what to change, and what to release.

Wisdom emerges when patterns are recognized. Repeated pain points indicate unresolved needs. Darkness points toward areas requiring attention.

This wisdom guides future choices. You make decisions informed by experience rather than avoidance. Healing reshapes direction.

Darkness, when engaged consciously, becomes a teacher rather than a burden.

Reclaiming Wholeness Through Acceptance

Wholeness does not require eliminating darkness. It requires accepting its place within the larger self. Healing through darkness restores coherence by integrating all parts of experience.

Acceptance does not mean approval of harm. It means acknowledging what happened and how it affected you. Resistance prolongs suffering; acceptance allows movement.

When acceptance occurs, the internal struggle decreases. Energy once spent suppressing pain becomes available for growth. You feel more grounded, less fragmented.

Wholeness supports resilience. You are no longer destabilized by emotional complexity. You can hold contradiction without collapse.

Healing is not becoming someone new—it is becoming more fully yourself.

Dark Self's Advice

Stop trying to fix me. I don't need repair—I need permission to exist. When you listen instead of correcting, I show you where healing actually lives.

I carry pain because no one helped you carry it then. Sit with me now. You don't have to relive anything—just stay present long enough for the weight to shift.

Exercises

Exercise 1: Compassionate Witnessing

1. Identify a painful memory or emotion.
2. Sit quietly and notice where it lives in your body.
3. Place a hand on that area and breathe slowly.
4. Offer a compassionate statement to that part of yourself.

Exercise 2: Boundary Repair

1. Identify a situation where your needs were ignored.
2. Write what you wish you had said or done.
3. Practice expressing that boundary aloud in a safe space.

Exercise 3: Integration Statement

1. Write about a pain that shaped you.
2. Identify what it taught you.
3. Write a statement acknowledging both the pain and the strength gained.

Journal Prompts

1. What pain do I avoid revisiting?
2. What part of me learned to endure silently?
3. How do I respond to my own suffering?
4. What coping strategy no longer serves me?
5. Where do I judge my past self?
6. What does compassion feel like in my body?
7. What wisdom has pain offered me?
8. How do I define healing?
9. What would acceptance change?
10. What does wholeness look like for me now?

Closing Reflection

Healing through darkness is not an act of courage alone—it is an act of loyalty to yourself. When you allow pain to be seen without judgment, it loosens its hold. Darkness does not disappear when healed; it transforms into depth, clarity, and strength. Wholeness is built not by erasing what hurt, but by integrating it with care and intention.

Chapter 6: Shadow Integration for Spiritual Growth

The Sacred Darkness Within the Cycle

In pagan and Wiccan traditions, darkness is not feared—it is honored. The dark half of the cycle is where seeds germinate, roots strengthen, and unseen forces prepare transformation. Shadow integration follows this same natural law. Growth does not occur only under sunlight; it begins in the soil.

The shadow is the spiritual compost of the self. It holds experiences broken down by time, emotion, and memory, ready to nourish something new. What was buried was not discarded—it was planted. Spiritual growth depends on whether you tend this inner ground consciously.

To reject the shadow is to reject half of the Wheel. Light without darkness becomes brittle, performative, and disconnected from lived truth. Pagan spirituality understands balance not as moral purity, but as harmony between opposing forces.

Shadow integration is a sacred act because it restores wholeness. It aligns the inner world with the rhythms of nature: waxing and waning, descent and return. You are not meant to transcend your darkness—you are meant to walk with it.

When the shadow is honored, spiritual growth becomes embodied rather than abstract.

The Shadow as the Wild Self

The shadow carries the wild self—the instinctual, intuitive, and untamed aspects of your spirit. This is the part of you that senses truth before language, that knows when boundaries are crossed, that responds to energy rather than explanation.

Modern life often suppresses the wild self in favor of predictability and control. Yet pagan paths recognize wildness as sacred intelligence. The shadow preserves this intelligence when it cannot be expressed openly.

Integration allows the wild self to return with structure. It is not chaos—it is instinct refined by awareness. The wild self does not seek destruction; it seeks alignment.

When honored, this aspect sharpens intuition, deepens ritual, and strengthens energetic boundaries. You stop outsourcing authority to external rules and begin listening inward.

Spiritual growth accelerates when instinct and intention are woven together.

Ritual as a Bridge Between Conscious and Shadow

Ritual is one of the most powerful tools for shadow integration. Unlike purely cognitive practices, ritual speaks the language of the subconscious and the spirit. It uses symbol, movement, and intention to access what words cannot reach.

Shadow-focused ritual does not banish darkness—it invites it into sacred space. Circles are cast not to exclude parts of the self, but to create safety for honest encounter. Candles, stones, earth, and breath anchor the work.

In ritual, the shadow is witnessed rather than analyzed. Emotions are allowed form. Energy is directed with purpose. This transforms raw experience into spiritual insight.

Ritual teaches the shadow that it is welcome. When the shadow feels safe, it reveals wisdom rather than resistance.

Through ritual, integration becomes communion.

Alchemy of Shadow and Light

Pagan spirituality often speaks of alchemy—not as the pursuit of perfection, but as transformation through union. Shadow integration is inner alchemy. Darkness and light are not opposites to be reconciled, but forces to be blended.

When shadow traits are integrated, they change quality. Anger becomes protection. Desire becomes devotion. Fear becomes discernment. This is spiritual maturation, not moral correction.

Alchemy requires patience. Quick fixes fracture the process. Integration unfolds through repeated attention, reflection, and ritual engagement. Each cycle deepens understanding.

The alchemical self is not purified—it is tempered. Strength comes from having been shaped by heat, pressure, and time.

Spiritual growth is not ascent alone—it is descent and return.

Ancestral Memory and the Shadow

The shadow does not belong to you alone. It carries ancestral memory—patterns, fears, and strengths passed through blood and story. Pagan traditions honor this inheritance rather than denying it.

Some shadow material arises not from personal experience, but from collective survival. Scarcity, vigilance, and resilience echo through generations. Integration allows you to choose which inheritances to keep.

Honoring ancestors does not mean repeating their wounds. It means acknowledging their influence and releasing what no longer serves the present cycle.

Shadow work becomes ancestral healing when you consciously interrupt harmful patterns and embody new ones. This is sacred responsibility.

When you integrate your shadow, you shift the lineage forward.

Living as a Whole Spiritual Being

Shadow integration is not confined to ritual space. It is lived through choices, boundaries, and self-respect. Spiritual growth becomes practical when the shadow is integrated.

You stop seeking external validation for inner truth. You trust your intuition without abandoning discernment. You act in alignment even when it is uncomfortable.

Wholeness allows spiritual practice to deepen without dissociation. You remain grounded in the body, the land, and the present moment. The sacred is not elsewhere—it is here.

Living integrated means honoring both the hearth fire and the night sky. Stillness and intensity. Softness and ferocity.

This is pagan spirituality embodied—not escaped into, but lived.

Dark Self's Advice

I am not the opposite of your spirituality—I am its root. I hold what you buried when you were taught to be smaller, quieter, safer. When you honor me, your magic becomes real.

Stop reaching upward without grounding downward. Sit with me in the dark soil. I will show you how to grow without breaking.

Exercises

Exercise 1: Shadow Candle Rite

1. Light a black or dark-colored candle.
2. Speak aloud one shadow trait you avoid.
3. Name how it once protected you.
4. Sit in silence, feeling its presence without judgment.

Exercise 2: Wild Self Invocation

1. Go outdoors or near a window.
2. Place your hands on the earth or floor.
3. Ask inwardly: "What instinct do I need to trust?"
4. Write what arises without filtering.

Exercise 3: Ancestral Release Practice

1. Identify a repeating pattern in your life.
2. Acknowledge it as inherited, not personal failure.
3. Speak a release statement, offering gratitude and closure.

Journal Prompts

1. What darkness do I resist spiritually?
2. What instincts feel forbidden?
3. How do I relate to the cycles of descent?
4. What part of me feels wild?
5. What ancestral patterns do I recognize?
6. Where do I seek light to avoid truth?
7. How does my body signal intuition?
8. What shadow trait strengthens my magic?
9. What does balance mean to me?
10. How do I live my spirituality daily?

Closing Reflection

Shadow integration is not a detour from spiritual growth—it is the path itself. Pagan wisdom teaches that nothing sacred is separated from the earth, the body, or the dark. When you honor the shadow, your spirituality becomes rooted, resilient, and real. You do not rise by rejecting the dark—you rise because you walked through it whole.

Chapter 7: The Connection Between Magick and the Shadow Self

Magick as the Art of Inner Alignment

Magick, in pagan understanding, is not about domination over forces—it is about alignment with them. True magick begins within, where intention, emotion, belief, and will converge. The shadow self plays a central role in this convergence because it contains the energies most often denied conscious expression.

When magick fails or feels hollow, it is often because the practitioner is fragmented. Words are spoken, tools are arranged, but the shadow is excluded. Suppressed fear, anger, desire, or doubt creates energetic contradiction. The spell says one thing; the shadow believes another.

The shadow does not sabotage magick out of spite. It resists being ignored. If a part of you does not believe you deserve the outcome, or fears the consequence of change, that resistance becomes part of the working.

Magick responds to wholeness. When conscious intention and shadow truth align, energy flows cleanly. Power sharpens. Results stabilize.

Shadow integration is not optional for effective magick—it is foundational.

The Shadow as the Source of Raw Power

The shadow holds the densest forms of personal energy. Anger, grief, longing, lust, and fear are potent forces. They move the body, focus the mind, and command attention. Pagan magick does not reject these forces—it teaches how to shape them.

Many traditions recognize that emotion is fuel. Cold, detached intention lacks momentum. Shadow emotions, when acknowledged and directed, become propulsion. They give spells weight and direction.

Fear refines clarity. Anger defines boundaries. Desire creates momentum. These energies are dangerous only when unconscious. Integrated, they are precise.

The shadow is where your personal power has been stored. It accumulated there because it was not allowed expression elsewhere. Magick provides a container for its release and transformation.

When you stop fearing your shadow, your magick stops leaking energy.

Why Avoided Emotions Weaken Spellwork

Avoidance creates energetic contradiction. If you cast for protection while suppressing rage, the spell is diluted. If you cast for abundance while hiding shame around desire, the working fractures.

Magick amplifies what is present, not what is performed. Ritual does not override inner truth—it reveals it. This is why shadow work often precedes stronger results.

Avoided emotions continue operating beneath the surface. They influence timing, confidence, and follow-through. The practitioner may blame external forces when the disruption is internal.

Acknowledging shadow emotions before spellwork stabilizes intention. It allows you to choose which energies to channel rather than being hijacked by them.

Honesty strengthens magick more than positivity ever could.

Ritual as Shadow Communion

Ritual is a meeting place between conscious will and shadow truth. Circles are not only protective—they are invitational. They mark a space where all parts of the self are allowed presence.

Shadow-focused ritual invites honesty. Candles lit for grief, anger named aloud, desires spoken without apology. This does not pollute the ritual—it completes it.

In ritual space, the shadow is not judged. It is witnessed. This witnessing transforms raw emotion into usable energy. What was chaotic becomes intentional.

Over time, the shadow learns it has a voice. It no longer needs to disrupt from the background. Ritual becomes communion rather than performance.

Magick deepens when every part of you is invited to the circle.

Ethics, Responsibility, and Integrated Will

Pagan magick emphasizes responsibility over obedience. Without shadow integration, ethics become brittle or performative. A practitioner may claim restraint while acting unconsciously from resentment or fear.

Integrated shadow clarifies ethical boundaries. You understand your motives. You recognize when desire seeks expression and when it seeks avoidance. This self-knowledge prevents unconscious harm.

Will, when integrated, becomes steady rather than forceful. You no longer need to overpower reality—you collaborate with it. Your workings become cleaner and less reactive.

Shadow integration does not make magick darker—it makes it more accountable. You own your power rather than displacing it.

Ethical magick begins with internal honesty.

Living Magick Through Shadow Awareness

Magick is not confined to ritual. It is lived through daily choices, boundaries, and responses. Shadow awareness ensures that your lived magick matches your ritual intent.

When shadow and conscious self are aligned, your presence becomes magnetic. Words carry weight. Actions follow intention. The mundane becomes enchanted through coherence.

You stop compartmentalizing spirituality. Magick becomes embodied rather than symbolic. The shadow informs intuition, timing, and discernment.

Living magick is the result of integration. You do not switch power on and off—you inhabit it.

This is the difference between practicing magick and *being* magickal.

Dark Self's Advice

You keep asking why your spells feel weak. It's because you whisper intentions while I'm screaming truths. Invite me in, and I'll stop pulling the energy sideways.

I am not dangerous to your magick—I am its engine. Use me consciously, or I will use myself unconsciously.

Exercises

Exercise 1: Shadow Check-In Before Spellwork

1. Before any ritual, write down what you are feeling honestly.
2. Name any resistance, fear, or doubt present.
3. Decide whether to include or postpone the working based on clarity.

Exercise 2: Emotion-as-Fuel Practice

1. Choose a strong emotion you usually suppress.
2. Sit with it and feel it fully without acting.
3. Visualize it flowing into a simple intention (clarity, protection, grounding).

Exercise 3: Post-Ritual Shadow Review

1. After a ritual, journal how you actually felt during it.
2. Note any moments of discomfort or distraction.
3. Reflect on what shadow aspect was present.

Journal Prompts

1. What emotions do I avoid in ritual?
2. Where do my spells feel blocked?
3. What truth am I afraid magick will reveal?
4. How do I feel about my own power?
5. What shadow trait strengthens my workings?
6. When has honesty changed a ritual outcome?
7. What desire feels unsafe to name?
8. Where do ethics feel performative?
9. How does my body respond during spellwork?
10. What would change if I trusted my shadow?

Closing Reflection

Magick does not separate light from dark—it weaves them. When the shadow is excluded, power fractures. When it is integrated, magick becomes grounded, ethical, and alive. The shadow is not a flaw in your practice—it is the current beneath it. When you work with it consciously, your magick stops being something you do and becomes something you *are*.

Chapter 8: The Myths and Archetypes of the Dark Side

Why Myth Is the Language of the Shadow

The shadow does not speak in facts or formulas. It speaks in image, symbol, and story. Myth is the oldest language of the shadow because it was born before psychology, before doctrine, before moral absolutism. Myth gave form to inner experiences humans could not otherwise explain.

In Wiccan and pagan traditions, myths are not lessons about good versus evil. They are maps of transformation. Dark figures exist not to be defeated, but to be encountered. They mark thresholds: initiation, loss, descent, and rebirth.

When modern minds reject myth as fiction, they lose access to symbolic intelligence. The shadow continues to communicate—but without shared language, its messages feel chaotic or threatening. Myth restores coherence.

Each archetype represents a pattern that exists within you. You do not worship these figures as external authorities—you recognize them as inner forces reflected outward. Myth becomes a mirror, not a commandment.

Shadow work deepens when you realize you are not inventing your darkness—you are remembering it.

The Descent as Sacred Pattern

One of the most consistent mythic patterns is descent. The goddess descends into the underworld. The initiate enters darkness. The seed is buried. These stories appear across pagan cultures because they reflect an unavoidable truth: growth requires descent.

The dark side is where identity dissolves and reforms. It strips illusion, exposes fear, and confronts limitation. This is not punishment—it is preparation. Without descent, power remains untested and shallow.

Modern spirituality often tries to bypass descent, chasing transcendence without grounding. Pagan myth rejects this. You cannot rise without first going down. The shadow is the gatekeeper of depth.

Descent myths teach surrender without annihilation. The self that enters darkness is not the self that returns. Something is shed. Something is claimed.

Shadow integration follows this same rhythm. You are not broken—you are mid-cycle.

The Dark Feminine as Sovereignty, Not Submission

The dark feminine in Wiccan myth is not passive, corrupted, or fallen. She is sovereign. She chooses when to nurture and when to destroy. She governs thresholds: birth, death, sexuality, rage, and rebirth.

This archetype frightens systems built on control because she cannot be dominated. She does not seek approval. She acts from inner authority. The shadow self resonates deeply with this figure because it, too, resists suppression.

The dark feminine teaches boundaries through consequence. She does not negotiate endlessly. She withdraws, withholds, or transforms when crossed. This is not cruelty—it is balance.

Within you, this archetype lives wherever you stop explaining yourself. Wherever you say no without apology. Wherever you honor instinct over expectation.

Shadow work awakens this sovereignty gently or violently, depending on how long it has been denied.

The Dark Masculine as Guardian of Thresholds

The dark masculine in pagan myth is not tyranny or domination—it is containment, protection, and decisive force. He stands at gates. He enforces boundaries. He acts when deliberation ends.

This archetype is often misunderstood because power without tenderness is feared. But the dark masculine is not reckless—it is resolute. It knows when something must end so something else may live.

In the shadow self, this archetype emerges as assertiveness, clarity, and refusal to be diminished. When suppressed, it becomes aggression or collapse. When integrated, it becomes steady authority.

The dark masculine does not seek control over others. It seeks responsibility for self. It acts not from ego, but from alignment.

Shadow integration refines this force into grounded strength.

The Witch as the Integrated Shadow

The Witch archetype is the meeting point of shadow and will. She knows the dark and the light because she has walked both. She does not deny her shadow—she uses it consciously.

In myth, the Witch is feared because she is not split. She feels deeply and thinks clearly. She holds grief, rage, desire, and wisdom without fragmentation. This makes her powerful.

The Witch understands cycles. She knows when to act and when to wait. She does not rush healing or transformation. She trusts the timing of descent and return.

Within shadow work, the Witch represents integration. When you stop moralizing your inner world and start working with it, this archetype awakens.

You do not become the Witch by learning spells—you become her by knowing yourself.

The Dark Side as Initiation, Not Corruption

In Wiccan myth, darkness initiates—it does not damn. To encounter the dark side is to be tested, not condemned. Initiation asks: Can you hold truth without collapse? Can you wield power without denial?

The shadow self is the initiator within. It brings challenges that force honesty. It strips false identities. It demands accountability for desire and action.

Those who refuse initiation remain fragmented. Those who accept it emerge whole. This is the difference between spiritual performance and spiritual maturity.

The dark side is not something you escape. It is something you pass through, carrying what is real and shedding what is not.

Initiation ends when you stop running.

Wiccan Archetypes of the Dark Side

The Crone – Keeper of endings, truth, and hard-earned wisdom. She governs death, release, and clarity without illusion.

The Dark Goddess – Sovereign of the underworld and the womb. She embodies transformation, rage, sexuality, and rebirth.

The Horned God (Shadow Aspect) – Guardian of wild instinct, boundaries, and primal will. He governs hunt, sacrifice, and survival.

The Witch – Integrated wielder of shadow and will. She represents self-knowledge, personal power, and conscious magick.

The Initiate – The one who descends willingly. This archetype governs surrender, fear, and becoming.

The Gatekeeper – The force that tests readiness. It appears as fear, resistance, or obstacle before transformation.

Dark Self's Advice

You keep asking which archetype you are, but you've lived all of them. I am the part of you that remembers when to descend and when to rise. Stop trying to choose light over dark—they belong together.

I am not here to scare you. I am here to initiate you. Meet me honestly, and you won't need myth to explain me—I will live through you.

Exercises

Exercise 1: Archetype Recognition

1. Read through the archetypes slowly.
2. Identify which one provokes the strongest emotional response.
3. Write how this archetype appears in your life right now.

Exercise 2: Descent Visualization

1. Close your eyes and imagine descending into a dark sacred space.
2. Notice which archetype meets you there.
3. Ask what it wants you to learn.

Exercise 3: Archetypal Integration Statement

1. Choose one archetype you resist.
2. Write how it protects you.
3. Write one way to honor it consciously.

Journal Prompts

1. Which archetype frightens me most?
2. Where do I resist descent?
3. What power have I buried?
4. How do I relate to endings?
5. Where do I feel sovereign?
6. What instinct do I suppress?
7. What does initiation mean to me?
8. Which myth mirrors my life?
9. What truth am I avoiding?
10. What archetype am I becoming?

Closing Reflection

The dark side has never been without form, name, or purpose. Myth gave it shape so it could be honored rather than feared. When you recognize these archetypes within yourself, the shadow stops being chaos and becomes lineage. You are not inventing your path—you are walking one that has always existed, with eyes open and power integrated.

Chapter 9: Embracing the Shadow for Personal Power

Power Begins Where Denial Ends

Personal power does not emerge from perfection or control. It emerges from honesty. The moment you stop denying parts of yourself, energy that was bound in suppression becomes available. The shadow holds this energy because it has been guarding what you were told not to be.

Denial fragments power. When you disown anger, it controls you indirectly. When you deny desire, it distorts into obsession or withdrawal. Power leaks through the cracks created by rejection of self.

Embracing the shadow restores cohesion. Instead of fighting yourself, you align inner forces. This alignment generates strength that feels grounded rather than frantic. You move with intention instead of reaction.

Power rooted in shadow integration is quiet but unmistakable. It does not seek validation. It is not threatened by disagreement. It knows its boundaries and defends them without excess.

True power does not announce itself. It stabilizes the self from within.

Claiming Authority Over Your Inner World

Authority begins internally. Before you can act with confidence in the outer world, you must establish governance within. The shadow self often holds traits associated with authority—assertiveness, decisiveness, refusal—that were suppressed in the name of acceptance.

When these traits are denied, authority collapses outwardly. You may over-explain, hesitate, or seek permission. The shadow reacts by pushing harder, sometimes through resentment or abrupt behavior.

Embracing the shadow reclaims these traits consciously. You decide when to assert, when to withdraw, when to engage. Authority becomes choice rather than compulsion.

Internal authority creates consistency. You stop contradicting yourself. Your words, actions, and boundaries align. This coherence is felt by others immediately.

Power grows where inner governance is clear.

The Shadow as the Seat of Boundaries

Boundaries are not intellectual—they are energetic. The shadow stores the instinctual knowledge of where you end and others begin. When boundaries are violated, the shadow reacts before the mind does.

Many people are taught to override these signals. They rationalize discomfort or suppress anger to maintain harmony. Over time, boundaries erode, and power drains.

Embracing the shadow restores boundary awareness. You recognize discomfort as information rather than inconvenience. Anger becomes a messenger, not a threat.

Healthy boundaries are firm without being hostile. They do not require justification. The shadow teaches this clarity when allowed voice.

Personal power stabilizes when boundaries are honored without apology.

Transforming Suppressed Desire into Direction

Desire is often feared because it reveals hunger—want, ambition, longing. Suppressed desire does not disappear; it mutates. It shows up as envy, dissatisfaction, or numbness.

The shadow holds desire because desire threatens control structures. Embracing it requires honesty about what you want and what you are willing to do to obtain it ethically.

When desire is integrated, it becomes direction. You stop drifting. Decisions gain momentum. Effort aligns with intention.

Desire clarified by shadow work is not impulsive—it is focused. You choose consciously rather than reactively.

Power flows where desire is acknowledged and directed.

Power Without Performance

Many people confuse power with dominance, volume, or visibility. This is performance, not power. True power does not need constant reinforcement.

When the shadow is embraced, you stop performing strength. You stop proving worth. You become internally anchored. Silence gains weight. Stillness carries authority.

This power is resilient. It does not collapse under pressure or criticism. It adapts without losing core alignment.

Others may sense this shift without being able to name it. Your presence changes because you are no longer divided.

Power expressed without performance is sustainable.

Living From an Integrated Center

Integration creates a center of gravity. Decisions originate from within rather than from fear of external response. You act in alignment even when outcomes are uncertain.

The shadow becomes an advisor rather than an adversary. It informs timing, boundaries, and instinct. You listen without surrendering control.

Living from this center reduces inner conflict. Energy once spent managing contradiction becomes available for creation, protection, and growth.

This is not a final state—it is a practice. Integration deepens with use.

Personal power matures through consistent self-honesty.

Dark Self's Advice

You keep waiting for permission to be powerful. I was never waiting—I was contained. When you stop apologizing for your intensity, I stabilize instead of erupt.

Power isn't something you earn later. It's something you stop abandoning.

Exercises

Exercise 1: Power Inventory

1. List traits you associate with power.
2. Identify which of these you suppress.
3. Write how each suppressed trait could be expressed responsibly.

Exercise 2: Boundary Activation

1. Recall a recent boundary violation.
2. Write what your body felt before you reacted.
3. Practice stating a clear boundary aloud.

Exercise 3: Desire Clarification

1. Write one desire you avoid admitting.
2. Identify what fear is attached to it.
3. Define one ethical step toward it.

Journal Prompts

1. Where do I give my power away?
2. What intensity do I suppress?
3. When do I feel most aligned?
4. What boundary am I avoiding?
5. What desire feels dangerous?
6. How do I perform strength?
7. Where does fear override instinct?
8. What does authority mean to me?
9. When do I feel internally divided?
10. What would change if I trusted myself?

Closing Reflection

Embracing the shadow does not make you harder—it makes you whole. Personal power is not domination or control; it is coherence. When you stop fragmenting yourself to be accepted, power returns naturally. The shadow does not create power—it restores what was always yours.

Chapter 10: Walking the Path of Balance

Balance as a Living Practice

Balance is not a destination you reach and remain within. It is a living practice—responsive, dynamic, and shaped by circumstance. In pagan understanding, balance mirrors the natural world: tides rise and fall, seasons turn, light waxes and wanes. Stability comes not from stillness, but from movement held with awareness.

Walking the path of balance means abandoning extremes. It is not light denying dark, nor dark overwhelming light. It is the continual negotiation between instinct and reflection, action and rest, expression and restraint. Balance lives in the *between*.

Many people search for balance as a feeling of calm or neutrality. In reality, balance often feels active. It requires attention, adjustment, and humility. When life shifts, balance must shift with it.

The shadow plays a crucial role here. It alerts you when imbalance grows—when boundaries weaken, when suppression builds, when desire is ignored. Without the shadow's signals, balance becomes illusion.

True balance is not comfort. It is alignment maintained through awareness.

The Dance Between Light and Shadow

Light and shadow are not opposing forces competing for dominance. They are partners in a sacred dance. Light brings clarity, insight, and expansion. Shadow brings depth, instinct, and truth. One without the other becomes distorted.

Excessive light leads to denial—spiritual bypassing, false positivity, avoidance of discomfort. Excessive shadow leads to overwhelm—rumination, fixation, loss of perspective. Balance emerges when each is given its role.

In Wiccan paths, the Wheel of the Year teaches this dance clearly. Growth requires both planting and decay. Celebration follows mourning. Power rests in honoring each phase without clinging.

Walking the balanced path means knowing when to illuminate and when to descend. When to speak and when to listen. When to act and when to wait.

The shadow does not disrupt balance—it restores it when ignored.

Self-Regulation as Sacred Skill

Balance depends on self-regulation—the ability to respond rather than react. This skill is not suppression. It is attunement. You sense internal shifts and adjust before extremes take hold.

The shadow informs regulation by signaling unmet needs. Irritation may indicate a boundary breach. Fatigue may signal overextension. Desire may point toward stagnation. Ignoring these cues leads to imbalance.

Regulation requires honesty. You must be willing to admit when something is off without immediately fixing or judging it. This pause creates space for wise response.

In pagan practice, regulation mirrors ritual containment. A circle holds energy so it can be directed safely. Self-regulation creates an inner circle where emotions can move without causing harm.

Balance grows stronger when regulation becomes habitual.

Ethical Power and Measured Action

Power without balance becomes destructive. Balance without power becomes passive. Walking the path of balance integrates both—strength guided by discernment.

Ethical action arises when shadow awareness informs decision-making. You recognize your motives. You understand your capacity for harm as well as good. This knowledge tempers action with responsibility.

Balanced power does not rush. It assesses timing. It considers consequence. It acts decisively when necessary and withdraws when appropriate.

This measured approach prevents burnout and regret. You conserve energy by acting only when aligned. You stop forcing outcomes and start cooperating with circumstance.

Balance refines power into wisdom.

Sustaining Wholeness Over Time

Integration is not a single breakthrough—it is maintenance. Walking the path of balance means revisiting shadow work as life evolves. New experiences activate new layers.

Sustaining wholeness requires routine reflection. Checking in with yourself becomes as natural as checking the weather. You notice patterns before they harden.

Balance also requires forgiveness. You will drift. You will overextend or retreat too far. The practice is returning without self-punishment.

Over time, this return becomes easier. You recognize imbalance sooner. Recovery quickens. Wholeness stabilizes.

Balance is not fragile—it strengthens through repetition.

Balance as Devotion to the Self

Walking the path of balance is an act of devotion—not to perfection, but to truth. You commit to honoring all parts of yourself without letting any single part rule unchecked.

This devotion grounds spirituality in daily life. Choices become offerings. Boundaries become sacred acts. Rest becomes ritual.

You stop seeking external validation for inner alignment. Balance becomes self-confirming. You feel it in your body, your decisions, your relationships.

The path does not end. It deepens. Balance becomes less effortful as trust grows.

This is how the work becomes a way of living.

Dark Self's Advice

Don't mistake balance for silence. When I speak, it's because something is tipping. Listen early, and I won't need to shout.

I don't want control—I want cooperation. Walk with me, not against me, and we won't lose our footing.

Exercises

Exercise 1: Balance Scan

1. Sit quietly and scan your body for tension or heaviness.
2. Note which area feels overextended or neglected.
3. Write one small adjustment that restores equilibrium.

Exercise 2: Light–Shadow Dialogue

1. Write a question from your conscious self.
2. Let your shadow respond honestly.
3. Write a balanced response that honors both perspectives.

Exercise 3: Cycle Awareness Practice

1. Identify a phase you are currently in (growth, rest, release).
2. Write how you are resisting or honoring it.
3. Choose one action that aligns with the phase.

Journal Prompts

1. Where am I out of balance?
2. What signal am I ignoring?
3. How do I respond to extremes?
4. What does balance feel like in my body?
5. Where do I overcorrect?
6. What phase am I resisting?
7. How do I regulate discomfort?
8. What part of me needs attention?
9. Where does power feel steady?
10. What helps me return to center?

Closing Reflection

Walking the path of balance is not about holding still—it is about moving with awareness. When light and shadow are honored together, life becomes navigable rather than chaotic. Balance is the quiet strength that emerges when you stop choosing sides within yourself and start walking forward whole.

Appendix A: Six Exercises for Integrating the Shadow Self

This appendix is designed as a **practical integration companion** to the work you've done throughout this book. These exercises are not meant to be rushed or completed all at once. Shadow integration unfolds through repetition, honesty, and patience. Return to these practices as often as needed, especially during periods of emotional charge, transition, or spiritual deepening.

Each exercise is written to engage the **mind, body, and subconscious**, honoring the pagan understanding that transformation occurs through embodied awareness rather than force.

Exercise 1: The Shadow Naming Rite

Purpose:

To remove fear and vagueness by giving conscious language to shadow aspects.

Steps:

1. Sit in a quiet space where you will not be interrupted.
2. Write the question: *"What part of myself do I avoid acknowledging?"*
3. Allow words or traits to surface without editing (anger, envy, hunger, resentment, intensity, fear, etc.).
4. Choose one trait and write it clearly at the top of the page.
5. Beneath it, write how this trait has shown up indirectly in your life.
6. Finish by writing one sentence acknowledging this trait without judgment (example: *"This part of me exists because it learned how to survive."*).

Integration Focus:

Naming reduces distortion. What is named becomes manageable.

Exercise 2: Body-Based Shadow Listening

Purpose:

To access shadow material stored in physical sensation rather than thought.

Steps:

1. Sit or lie down comfortably. Close your eyes.
2. Take five slow breaths, allowing your body to settle.
3. Scan your body from head to toe, noticing areas of tension, heaviness, or numbness.
4. When you find a sensation that draws attention, rest awareness there.
5. Ask inwardly: *"What emotion or message lives here?"*
6. Do not force an answer—notice impressions, words, or images.
7. Afterward, write what you experienced without interpretation.

Integration Focus:

The body speaks before the mind understands. Listening builds trust.

Exercise 3: Shadow Dialogue Writing

Purpose:

To establish conscious communication with the shadow self.

Steps:

1. Divide a page into two columns.
2. Label the left column **Conscious Self** and the right **Shadow Self**.
3. Begin by writing a question from the conscious self (e.g., *"Why do you keep showing up as anger?"*).
4. Respond from the shadow without filtering or censoring.
5. Continue the dialogue for at least 10 exchanges.
6. End by writing one sentence of acknowledgment from the conscious self.

Integration Focus:

Dialogue transforms opposition into cooperation.

Exercise 4: Trigger-to-Truth Mapping

Purpose:

To convert emotional triggers into insight rather than reaction.

Steps:

1. Recall a recent situation that provoked a strong emotional response.
2. Write a brief description of the event.
3. Identify the immediate emotion felt (anger, shame, fear, jealousy, etc.).
4. Ask: *"What boundary, desire, or value was activated?"*
5. Write what the reaction was trying to protect.
6. Identify one conscious response you could choose next time.

Integration Focus:

Triggers are not flaws—they are signals.

Exercise 5: Shadow Integration Ritual (Non-Dogmatic)

Purpose:

To integrate shadow awareness through ritual containment.

Steps:

1. Create a simple sacred space (candle, stone, earth, or object of meaning).
2. Sit quietly and state aloud: *"All parts of me are welcome in this space."*
3. Name one shadow trait you've been working with.
4. Place your hand over your heart or abdomen and breathe slowly for three minutes.
5. Visualize this trait settling into your body calmly rather than explosively.
6. Close by thanking yourself for the honesty.

Integration Focus:

Ritual gives the shadow a safe place to exist consciously.

Exercise 6: Shadow-to-Strength Reframing

Purpose:

To transform shadow traits into usable personal power.

Steps:

1. Choose one shadow trait you judge harshly.
2. Write how it has caused difficulty when unconscious.
3. Write how this same trait could serve you if integrated (anger → boundaries, fear → discernment, desire → direction).
4. Define one practical way to express this trait responsibly.
5. Commit to observing this expression over the next week.

Integration Focus:

The shadow is not eliminated—it is refined.

Closing Note for Appendix A

Integration is not about becoming lighter, calmer, or easier to manage. It is about becoming **whole**. These exercises are not tests or requirements—they are invitations. Return to them when resistance arises, when emotions intensify, or when your spiritual practice feels disconnected from daily life.

The shadow does not disappear through effort.

It integrates through **attention, honesty, and respect**.

And every time you choose awareness over avoidance, you walk further into your own power.

<u>Message from the Author:</u>

I hope you enjoyed this book, I love astrology and knew there was not a book such as this out on the shelf. I love metaphysical items as well. Please check out my other books:

-Life of Government Benefits

-My life of Hell

-My life with Hydrocephalus

-Red Sky

-World Domination:Woman's rule

-World Domination:Woman's Rule 2: The War

-Life and Banishment of Apophis: book 1

-The Kidney Friendly Diet

-The Ultimate Hemp Cookbook

-Creating a Dispensary(legally)

-Cleanliness throughout life: the importance of showering from childhood to adulthood.

-Strong Roots: The Risks of Overcoddling children

-Hemp Horoscopes: Cosmic Insights and Earthly Healing

- Celestial Hemp Navigating the Zodiac: Through the Green Cosmos

-Astrological Hemp: Aligning The Stars with Earth's Ancient Herb

-The Astrological Guide to Hemp: Stars, Signs, and Sacred Leaves

-Green Growth: Innovative Marketing Strategies for your Hemp Products and Dispensary

-Cosmic Cannabis

-Astrological Munchies

-Henry The Hemp

-Zodiacal Roots: The Astrological Soul Of Hemp

- Green Constellations: Intersection of Hemp and Zodiac

-Hemp in The Houses: An astrological Adventure Through The Cannabis Galaxy

-Galactic Ganja Guide

Heavenly Hemp
Zodiac Leaves
Doctor Who Astrology
Cannastrology
Stellar Satvias and Cosmic Indicas
Celestial Cannabis: A Zodiac Journey
AstroHerbology: The Sky and The Soil: Volume 1
AstroHerbology:Celestial Cannabis:Volume 2
Cosmic Cannabis Cultivation
The Starry Guide to Herbal Harmony: Volume 1
The Starry Guide to Herbal Harmony: Cannabis Universe: Volume 2
Yugioh Astrology: Astrological Guide to Deck, Duels and more
Nightmare Mansion: Echoes of The Abyss
Nightmare Mansion 2: Legacy of Shadows
Nightmare Mansion 3: Shadows of the Forgotten
Nightmare Mansion 4: Echoes of the Damned
The Life and Banishment of Apophis: Book 2
Nightmare Mansion: Halls of Despair
Healing with Herb: Cannabis and Hydrocephalus
Planetary Pot: Aligning with Astrological Herbs: Volume 1
Fast Track to Freedom: 30 Days to Financial Independence Using AI, Assets, and Agile Hustles
Cosmic Hemp Pathways
How to Become Financially Free in 30 Days: 10,000 Paths to Prosperity
Zodiacal Herbage: Astrological Insights: Volume 1
Nightmare Mansion: Whispers in the Walls
The Daleks Invade Atlantis
Henry the hemp and Hydrocephalus

10X The Kidney Friendly Diet
Cannabis Universe: Adult coloring book

Hemp Astrology: The Healing Power of the Stars

Zodiacal Herbage: Astrological Insights: Cannabis Universe: Volume 2

Planetary Pot: Aligning with Astrological Herbs: Cannabis Universes: Volume 2

Doctor Who: Convergence Protocol – The Replicator War

Nightmare Mansion: Curse of the Blood Moon

The Celestial Stoner: A Guide to the Zodiac

Cosmic Pleasures: Sex Toy Astrology for Every Sign

Hydrocephalus Astrology: Navigating the Stars and Healing Waters

Lapis and the Mischievous Chocolate Bar

Celestial Positions: Sexual Astrology for Every Sign

Apophis's Shadow Work Journal: **:** A Journey of Self-Discovery and Healing

Kinky Cosmos: Sexual Kink Astrology for Every Sign

Digital Cosmos: The Astrological Digimon Compendium

Stellar Seeds: The Cosmic Guide to Growing with Astrology

Apophis's Daily Gratitude Journal

Cat Astrology: Feline Mysteries of the Cosmos

The Cosmic Kama Sutra: An Astrological Guide to Sexual Positions

Unleash Your Potential: A Guided Journal Powered by AI Insights

Whispers of the Enchanted Grove

Cosmic Pleasures: An Astrological Guide to Sexual Kinks

369, 12 Manifestation Journal

Whisper of the nocturne journal(blank journal for writing or drawing)

The Boogey Book

Locked In Reflection: A Chastity Journey Through Locktober

Generating Wealth Quickly:How to Generate $100,000 in 24 Hours

Star Magic: Harness the Power of the Universe

The Flatulence Chronicles: A Fart Journal for Self-Discovery

The Doctor and The Death Moth

Seize the Day: A Personal Seizure Tracking Journal

The Ultimate Boogeyman Safari: A Journey into the Boogie World and Beyond

Whispers of Samhain: 1,000 Spells of Love, Luck, and Lunar Magic: Samhain Spell Book

Apophis's guides:Witch's Spellbook Crafting Guide for Halloween

Frost & Flame: The Enchanted Yule Grimoire of 1000 Winter Spells

The Ultimate Boogey Goo Guide & Spooky Activities for Halloween Fun

Harmony of the Scales: A Libra's Spellcraft for Balance and Beauty

The Enchanted Advent: 36 Days of Christmas Wonders

Nightmare Mansion: The Labyrinth of Screams

Harvest of Enchantment: 1,000 Spells of Gratitude, Love, and Fortune for Thanksgiving

The Boogey Chronicles: A Journal of Nightly Encounters and Shadowy Secrets

The 12 Days of Financial Freedom: A Step-by-Step Christmas Countdown to Transform Your Finances

Sigil of the Eternal Spiral Blank Journal

A Christmas Feast: Timeless Recipes for Every Meal

Holiday Stress-Free Solutions: A Survival Guide to Thriving During the Festive Season

Yu-Gi-Oh! Holiday Gifting Mastery: The Ultimate Guide for Fans and Newcomers Alike

Holiday Harmony: A Hydrocephalus Survival Guide for the Festive Season

Celestial Craft: The Witch's Almanac for 2025 – A Cosmic Guide to Manifestations, Moons, and Mystical Events

Doctor Who: The Toymaker's Winter Wonderland

Tulsa King Unveiled: A Thrilling Guide to Stallone's Mafia Masterpiece

Pendulum Craft: A Complete Guide to Crafting and Using Personalized Divination Tools

Nightmare Mansion: Santa's Eternal Eve

Starlight Noel: A Cosmic Journey through Christmas Mysteries

The Dark Architect: Unlocking the Blueprint of Existence

Surviving the Embrace: The Ultimate Guide to Encounters with The Hugging Molly

The Enchanted Codex: Secrets of the Craft for Witches, Wiccans, and Pagans

Harvest of Gratitude: A Complete Thanksgiving Guide

Yuletide Essentials: A Complete Guide to an Authentic and Magical Christmas

Celestial Smokes: A Cosmic Guide to Cigars and Astrology

Living in Balance: A Comprehensive Survival Guide to Thriving with Diabetes Insipidus

Cosmic Symbiosis: The Venom Zodiac Chronicles

The Cursed Paw of Ambition

Cosmic Symbiosis: The Astrological Venom Journal

Celestial Wonders Unfold: A Stargazer's Guide to the Cosmos (2024-2029)

The Ultimate Black Friday Prepper's Guide: Mastering Shopping Strategies and Savings

Cosmic Sales: The Astrological Guide to Black Friday Shopping

Legends of the Corn Mother and Other Harvest Myths

Whispers of the Harvest: The Corn Mother's Journal

The Evergreen Spellbook

The Doctor Meets the Boogeyman

The White Witch of Rose Hall's SpellBook

The Gingerbread Golem's Shadow: A Study in Sweet Darkness

The Gingerbread Golem Codex: An Academic Exploration of Sweet Myths

The Gingerbread Golem Grimoire: Sweet Magicks and Spells for the Festive Witch

The Curse of the Gingerbread Golem

10-minute Christmas Crafts for kids

Christmas Crisis Solutions: The Ultimate Last-Minute Survival Guide

Gingerbread Golem Recipes: Holiday Treats with a Magical Twist

The Infinite Key: Unlocking Mystical Secrets of the Ages

Enchanted Yule: A Wiccan and Pagan Guide to a Magical and Memorable Season

Dinosaurs of Power: Unlocking Ancient Magick

Astro-Dinos: The Cosmic Guide to Prehistoric Wisdom

Gallifrey's Yule Logs: A Festive Doctor Who Cookbook

The Dino Grimoire: Secrets of Prehistoric Magick

The Gift They Never Knew They Needed

The Gingerbread Golem's Culinary Alchemy: Enchanting Recipes for a Sweetly Dark Feast

A Time Lord Christmas: Holiday Adventures with the Doctor

Krampusproofing Your Home: Defensive Strategies for Yule

Silent Frights: A Collection of Christmas Creepypastas to Chill Your Bones

Santa Raptor's Jolly Carnage: A Dino-Claus Christmas Tale

Prehistoric Palettes: A Dino Wicca Coloring Journey

The Christmas Wishkeeper Chronicles

The Starlight Sleigh: A Holiday Journey

Elf Secrets: The True Magic of the North Pole

Candy Cane Conjurations

Cooking with Kids: Recipes Under 20 Minutes

Doctor Who: The TARDIS Confiscation

The Anxiety First Aid Kit: Quick Tools to Calm Your Mind

Frosty Whispers: A Winter's Tale

The Infinite Key: Unlocking the Secrets to Prosperity, Resilience, and Purpose

The Grasping Void: Why You'll Regret This Purchase

Astrology for Busy Bees: Star Signs Simplified

The Instant Focus Formula: Cut Through the Noise

The Secret Language of Colors: Unlocking the Emotional Codes

Sacred Fossil Chronicles: Blank Journal

The Christmas Cottage Miracle

Feeding Frenzy: Graboid-Inspired Recipes

Manifest in Minutes: The Quick Law of Attraction Guide

The Symbiote Chronicles: Doctor Who's Venomous Journey

Think Tiny, Grow Big: The Minimalist Mindset

The Energy Key: Unlocking Limitless Motivation

New Year, New Magic: Manifesting Your Best Year Yet

Unstoppable You: Mastering Confidence in Minutes

Infinite Energy: The Secret to Never Feeling Drained

Lightning Focus: Mastering the Art of Productivity in a Distracted World

Saturnalia Manifestation Magick: A Guide to Unlocking Abundance During the Solstice

Graboids and Garland: The Ultimate Tremors-Themed Christmas Guide

12 Nights of Holiday Magic

The Power of Pause: 60-Second Mindfulness Practices

The Quick Reset: How to Reclaim Your Life After Burnout

The Shadow Eater: A Tale of Despair and Survival

The Micro-Mastery Method: Transform Your Skills in Just Minutes a Day

Reclaiming Time: How to Live More by Doing Less

Chronovore: The Eternal Nexus

The Mind Reset: Unlocking Your Inner Peace in a Chaotic World
Confidence Code: Building Unshakable Self-Belief
Baby the Vampire Terrier
Baby the Vampire Terrier's Christmas Adventure
Celestial Streams: The Content Creator's Astrology Manual
The Wealth Whisperer: Unlocking Abundance with Everyday Actions
The Energy Equation: Maximize Your Output Without Burning Out
The Happiness Algorithm: Science-Backed Steps to Joyful Living
Stress-Free Success: Achieving Goals Without Anxiety
Mindful Wealth: The New Blueprint for Financial Freedom
The Festive Flavors of New Year: A Culinary Celebration
The Master's Gambit: Keys of Eternal Power
Shadowed Secrets: Groundhog Day Mysteries
Beneath the Burrow: Lessons from the Groundhog
Spring's Whispers: The Groundhog's Prediction
The Limitless Mindset: Unlock Your Untapped Potential
The Focus Funnel: How to Cut Through Chaos and Get Results
Bold Moves: Building Courage to Live on Your Terms
The Daily Shift: Simple Practices for Lasting Transformation
The Quarter-Life Reset: Thriving in Your 20s and 30s
The Art of Shadowplay: Building Your Own Personal Myth
The Eternal Loop: Finding Purpose in Repetition
Burrowing Wisdom: Life Lessons from the Groundhog
Shadow Work: A Groundhog Day Perspective
Love in Bloom: 5-Minute Romantic Gestures
The Shadowspell Codex: Secrets of Forbidden Magick
The Burnout Cure: Finding Balance in a Busy World
The Groundhog Prophecy: Unlocking Seasonal Secrets
Nog Tales: The Spirited History of Eggnog
Six More Weeks: Embracing Seasonal Transitions
The Lumivian Chronicles: Fragments of the Fifth Dimension

Money on Your Mind: A Beginner's Guide to Wealth
The Focus Fix: Breaking Through Distraction
January's Spirit Keepers: Mystical Protectors of the Cold
Creativity Unchained: Unlocking Your Wildest Ideas in 2025
Manifestation Mastery: 365 Days to Rewrite Your Reality
The Groundhog's Mirror: Reflecting on Change
The Weeping Angels' Christmas Curse
Burrowed in Time: A Groundhog Day Journey
Heartbeats: Poems to Share with Your Valentine
Dino Wicca: The Sacred Grimoire of Prehistoric Magick
Courage of the Pride: Finding Your Inner Roar
The Lion's Leap: Bold Moves for Big Results
Healthy Hustle: Achieving Without Overworking
Practical Manifesting: Turning Dreams into Reality in 2025
Jurassic Pharaohs: Unlocking the Magick of Ancient Egypt and Dino Wicca
The Happiness Equation: Small Changes for Big Joy
The Confidence Compass: Finding Your Inner Strength
Whispers in the Hollow: Tales of the Forgotten Beasts
Echoes from the Hollow: The Return of Forgotten Beasts
The Hollow Ascendant: The Rise of the Forgotten Beasts
The Relationship Reset: Building Better Connections
Mastering the Morning: How to Win the Day Before 8 AM
The Shadow's Dance: Groundhog Day Symbolism
Cupid's Kitchen: Quick Valentine's Day Recipes
Valentine's Day on a Budget: Love Without Breaking the Bank
Astrocraft: Aligning the Stars in the World of Minecraft
Forecasting Life: Groundhog Day Reflections
Bleeding Hearts: Twisted Tales of Valentine's Terror
Herbal Smoke Revolution: The Ultimate Guide to Nature's Cigarette Alternative
Winter's Wrath: The Complete Survival Blueprint for Extreme Freezes.

The Groundhog's Shadow: A Tale of Seasons
Burrowed Insights: Wisdom from the Groundhog
Sensual Strings: The Art of Erotic Bondage
Whispered Flames: Unlocking the Power of Fire Play
Forgotten Shadows: A Guide to Cryptids Lost to Time
Six Weeks of Secrets: Groundhog Day's Hidden Messages
Shadows and Cycles: Groundhog Day Reflections
The Art of Love Letters: Crafting the Perfect Message
Romantic Getaways at Home: Turning Your Space into Paradise
Purrfect Brews: A Cat Lover's Guide to Coffee and Companionship
The Groundhog's Wisdom: Timeless Lessons for Modern Life
The Shadow Oracle: Groundhog Day as a Predictor
Emerging from the Burrow: A Journey of Renewal
The Language of Love: Learning Your Partner's Love Style
Authorpreneur: The Ultimate Blueprint for Writing, Publishing, and Thriving as an Author
Weathering the Seasons: Groundhog Day Perspectives
Valentine's Day Magic: A Guide to Romantic Rituals
The Shadow Chronicles: Stories of Groundhog Day
Love and Laughter: Fun Games for Valentine's Day
AstroRealty: Unlocking the Stars for Property Success
The Groundhog's Path: A Guide to Seasonal Balance
Groundhog Day Diaries: Reflections in the Shadow
The Groundhog's Light: Illuminating the Path Ahead
Valentine's Traditions from Around the World
AI Wealth Revolution: Unlocking the Trillionaire Mindset
Love Rekindled: Reigniting Passion in Relationships
Single and Thriving: Self-Love on Valentine's Day
Emerald Legends: Mystical Tales of Ireland
Green Alchemy: Harnessing Nature's Magic
The Hearts of Horror: A Valentine's Day Nightmare

The Leprechaun's Guide to Wealth and Wisdom
Dancing with the Sidhe: Celebrating the Otherworld
Shamrocks and Shadows: Mysteries of the Green Isle
Emerald Energy: Harnessing Luck and Growth
The Gingerbread Golem's Valentine: A Sweetheart's Guide to Love and Enchantment
The Celtic Knot: Weaving Life and Destiny
Green Fire: Elemental Magic for St. Patrick's Day
Clover Chronicles: Finding Your Inner Luck
Ireland's Mystical Creatures: A Field Guide
Gingerbread Golem's Love Almanac
Prowl and Thrive: The Lion's Guide to Success
Love Alchemy: Transforming Your Life Through Heart Energy
WORLD DOMINATION: Woman's Rule 3:The New Life
The Midnight Rose: A Guide to Lunar Love Spells
The Forbidden Letters: Writing Your Own Love Prophecy
Luck and Lore: St. Patrick's Day for Modern Mystics
The Green Path: A Pagan Celebration of Renewal
The Dark Architect's Guide to Reprogramming Reality
Prankster's Paradise: A Guide to Harmless Hijinks
Manifest Your Reality: The Law of Attraction Simplified
The TARDIS Owner's Manual: Understanding the Doctor's Ship: *A complete guide to the TARDIS, its technology, secrets, and mysteries*
Starlit Romance: Astrology Secrets for Finding True Love
The Time Lord's Atlas: A Complete Guide to the Whoniverse: ***A breakdown of the locations, planets, and dimensions explored in Doctor Who***
Sweetheart Shadows: The Dark Side of Love and Attraction
February Fire: Reigniting Passion in Every Area of Life
The Self-Love Toolkit: 5 Ways to Embrace Who You Are
February Sparks: Ignite Your Dreams in 28 Days

March to Success: A 31-Day Action Blueprint
Ancient Paths: The 13 Sacred Principles of Dino Wicca
Echoes of Tomorrow: Navigating the AI Revolution
The Wellness Blueprint: Balancing Mind, Body, and Soul
Green Horizons: Sustainable Living for a Better Tomorrow
The AI Wealth Code: How to Make Millions with Automation
AI-Powered Creativity: Writing, Art, and Music for Profit
Extinction Rites: Rebirthing Your Soul Through Prehistoric Magick
Sacred Serpents tarot
Celestial Enchantment blank journal
Star Strains
Culinary Journeys: Exploring Global Flavors at Home
The Hollowvale Curse
The Hollowvale Harvest
The Egg of Transformation: Awakening Your Inner Power
Blooming Into Power: A Wiccan Guide to Spring Awakening
The Nightmare Nexus: The Third Doctor's Perilous Haunting
Digital Detox: Reclaiming Your Life in a Connected World
Ostara's Path: Walking the Spiral of Renewal
The Sacred Hare
Financial Freedom: Building Wealth in the Modern Age
Spring's Cauldron: Stirring the Waters of Change
The Hollowvale Pact
Quantum Consciousness: The Science of Reality Shifting
The Hollowvale Hunger
The Sacred Waters Within: A Witch's Guide to Hydrocephalus Magick
The Raven's Nest: Building a Life of Unshakable Stability
AI and the Human Mind: The Future of Intelligence
The Hollowvale Reckoning
Timeless Love: Building and Maintaining Lasting Relationships

The Raven's Roar: Unlocking Unstoppable Confidence
Raven Sight: Awakening Intuition and Inner Wisdom
The Butterfly Effect: Small Changes, Big Transformations
Taming the Boogeyman: How to Conquer Your Inner Fears
The Magick of Green: Awakening Earth's Energy in You
The Entrepreneurial Mindset: Secrets to Business Success
The Hollowvale End
The Shadow Luck Ritual: Reclaiming Power from Your Dark Side
Spring Magick for Beginners: A Simple Guide to Seasonal Energy Work
Doctor Who: The Hollowvale Conundrum
The March of Miracles: Unlocking Synchronicities in Spring
Unveiling the Cosmos: A Guide to Stargazing and Space Exploration
The Ultimate Guide to Surviving an Economic Collapse
The AI Gold Rush: How to Profit from the AI Revolution
Bastet's Shadow: The Hidden Power of Feline Magick
The Bastet Codex: Unlocking the Goddess's Magickal Secrets
Purring Spells: Harnessing Bastet's Healing Frequencies
Bastet's Nine Lives: Rebirth, Transformation, and Immortality Spells
Primal Currents: Hydrocephalus Magick in the Path of Dino Wicca
The Digital Gold Rush: Mastering E-Commerce and Online Sales
Future Shock: Adapting to the Next Decade of Change
The Quantum Mindset: Think Like a Billionaire
Sacred Motherhood: Awakening the Divine Feminine Within
The Mother's Spellbook: Enchantments for Love, Protection, and Prosperity
The Witch's Guide to Parenting: Raising Empowered and Intuitive Children

The Magick of Motherhood: Reclaiming Your Power Through Rituals

The Pagan Path to Self-Love: A Goddess's Guide to Worth and Confidence

Wild Woman Magick: Unleashing Your Primal Power

The Money Magnet Blueprint: Unlocking Unlimited Wealth

Biohacking 101: Unlock Your Body's Full Potential

The Wild Father: A Pagan Guide to Strength and Wisdom

The Sacred Masculine: Unlocking Your Inner Power

The Druid's Compass

The Warrior's Mindset

The Father's Fire

Odin's Path

Ancestral Bonds

The House That Whispers

The Magician's Code

The Wild Hunt

The Green Man's Path

The Altar of Success

The Shadow and the Sword

The High Priestess's Guide to Energy Healing

The Lunar Mother

The Sacred Self-Care Grimoire

The Womb Wisdom Codex

The Wheel of the Mother

The Witch's Guide to Manifestation

The Q2 Reset

The Ultimate Guide to AI-Powered Passive Income

Escape the 9-5

AI Feline Fortunes

The Tear-Stained Grimoire

Razorblade Runes

Cemetery Sirens

The Midnight Wristwatch
The Town That Forgets
AI Horror & Creepypasta
The Hollow Frequency
The Breach Echo
The Quiet Between Worlds
The Sigil of Tharan-Khul
Summon the Vault of Y'ha'ten
The Becoming Codex
The Profit of Az'ra-nar
The Drowned Logos
Echoes of the Eldritch Will
The Deep Ledger
Necronomicon of Networth
Covenant of the Wealthwyrm
The Whisperer's Manifesto
The Rites of Azh-K'luth
The Ark of the Crawling Coin
The Tithe of Shadows
Inkheart Abyss
The Timewinds of Y'ha-nthlei
The Spiral Labyrinth of Azag-Nirrh
The Gallifreyan Heresy of the Black Pharaoh
The Psalms of Nyog-Sotha
Black Rain Alchemy
The Infinite Maw
The Entropic Blueprint
The Oracle of Sh'guul
The Book of Breach
The Drowned Saint's Testament
Dreamcraft of the Sleeper God
The Silence Market
Cthonomics: The Dark Wealth Algorithm

Invocation of the Ten-Eyed King
Wealthbound to the Wyrm Below
Become the Unnameable
Codex of the Sovereign Flame
Rituals of Relentless Becoming
The Shadow Ascends
The Eyes Beneath You
The Will That Wakes Worlds
Silence Is a Weapon
The Mirror That Screams
The Whisper Between Moments
The Mind That Devours Fear
The Myth of the Finished Self
The Architect of Your Madness
The Voice You've Buried
The Discipline of Madness
Stormborn: Awakening Your Inner Tempest
The Mind That Ate Time
Unbind Your Becoming
The Pact You Owe Yourself
The Devourer's Diet
The Acid That Carves the Path
The Tower You Must Burn
The Breath Between Worlds
Speak Like the Deep
The Labyrinth Within
The Spine of the Sea God
Rejection Is a Portal
The Crown You Refused
The Scar Is the Spell
The Lightless Flame
The Habit of Becoming Horrific
ChickenJockey Chaos

The Gatekeeper Within
You Are Not Your Name
The Compass of the Mad
The Archive of Unsent Letters
What the Mirror Can't Show You
The Knife You Needed
Worship Nothing, Become Everything
The Other Voice
The Body the World Forgot
The Vein of the Void
The Black Bone Codex
The Puzzle of the Hidden Self (Millennium Puzzle)
The Eye That Sees the Lie *(Millennium Eye)*
The Ring of Return (Millennium Ring)
The Rod of Relentless Will ***(Millennium Rod)***
The Tally of the Soul (Millennium Tauk/Necklace)
The Key to the Locked Timeline (Millennium Key)
The Scale of Sacred Decisions (Millennium Scales)
Inferno Bites: The UnOfficial Minecraft Lava Cookbook
Rot in the Attic
Prana: The Hidden Force of Your Infinite Self
The Shadow Realm Within: Transforming Darkness Into Destiny
The Borderland Collapse
Claws of Protection: Bastet's Defensive Magick
Mr. Ring-a-Ding's Madness
Yugioh Astrology: Celestial Deckcraft and Duel Destiny (2026–2027 Edition)
The Seal You Signed: Unlocking the Power You Once Feared
The Puzzle of Infinite Minds: Unlocking the Mentalism Hidden Within
The Eye That Mirrors the All: Secrets of Inner Reflection
Doctor Who: The Toymaker's Broadcast

The Rod of Eternal Flow: Commanding the Currents of Vibration
Golden Eyes of Bastet: Enhancing Psychic Vision
The Key of Dual Forces: Balance Within the Polarity
The Scales of Living Rhythm: Timing the Dance of Life
The Necklace of Hidden Cause: Weaving the Webs of Fate
The Ring of Secret Masters: Rising Through the All Within All
Daggers of the Dying Deep
Bastet's Wealth and Fortune Magick: Prosperity Rituals of the Goddess
The Tide that Speaks
The Scrolls of Petosiris: 13 Rituals from the Feathered Eye
Petosiris and the Living Plague of Osirion
Feline Fire: Bastet's Passion and Love Magick
The Star Altar of Petosiris
Bastet's Whiskers: Supernatural Sensory Magick
The Bastet Grimoire
Feeding the Shadows
The Mouthless Prayer
The Spiral Wound
Becoming the Ibis: Lessons from Petosiris's Mind
The Crimson Coven: Cola Magick for Sweet Dominion
Sacred Cat's Paw
The Soda Zodiac: A Flavor for Every Sign
Covenant of the Crawling Flame
The Ink of Ish'Zur
Frothroot: The Thirst That Ate the World
The Golden Glyphs of Prosperity
The Etherbind Codex
Echoes of the Resistance: Reclaiming the You That Survived
Harnessed Minds: Breaking Free from Mental Control
The Eyes in the Smoke

Rootwake: The Carbon Covenant
Skitter Logic: Unlearning the Fear That Built You
Doctor Who: The World That Froths
Rootwake: The Fizz That Rewrites Flesh
Rootwake: Frothfather of the World
The Holly Pact: Blood Beneath the Mistletoe
The 2nd Mass Principle: Building Unbreakable Tribes
Web of Wits: A Survival Guide to Encounters with Anasi the Spider (Aunt Nancy)
The Hexbreaking Handbook: Effective Spells to Remove Curses
Pop Alchemy: Transform Your Life One Sip at a Time
The Mason Code: Leading in Unleadable Times
Petosiris and the Fifth Chamber of Thoth
The Ether Seed Within
The Parent of Tomorrow
Petosiris's Pyramid of Perpetual Wealth
Unlearn the World
Grimoire of the Hollow Tongue
Zodiac Weeds: Finding Your Strain Through the Stars
Aquarius Rises in the Bank
The Sugar God's Smile
The Skinclock Reversal: Biohacking the Face of Time
Debtburn: How to Obliterate What You Owe Forever
The Ice Cream Oracle: What Your Cone Says About Your Future
Silence Is Sovereignty: The Power of Being Unreadable
The Wind That Whispers Through Stone
Path of the Four Directions
Doctor Who: The Maestro's Symphony of Endings
Oxygen Grail: Breathing to Undo the Clock
Zodiacal Collapse: When Stars Devour Time
Teachings from the Red Sand Silence

Doctor Who: Omega – The Broken Equation
Memory Wipe Your Past: Start Over Like a MiB
Mitochondria Prime: Ignite the Core of Youth
A Nest of Roaches
Grub from the Galaxy: MiB Recipes You'll Never Forget
Whiskers of Power: Bastet's Guide to Inner Sovereignty
The Gift Must Cost Them: Negotiation Through Unequal Exchange
The Worm Guys' Wealth Code: Hustle Like an Alien
Bug Out: The Edgar Method for Ruthless Goal Setting
Weaving Life with Spiderwoman's Pattern
Doctor Who: The Rani's Renaissance
How to Get a Job (If You're a Puppygirl)
Speak Through Others: The Art of Proxy Power
T-Rex Your Trauma: Reclaim the Power of Your Primal Self
The Black Briefcase: How MiB Stay Wealthy in Silence
The Thirst Beyond Reason: Understanding Diabetes Insipidus From the Inside Out
Backwoods Witchcraft for Billionaires: The Pagan Path from Dirt Roads to Gold Roads
The Moonshine Grimoire: Fermented Spells for Abundance
The Nameless Geometry
The Wraith's Mixtape: Spellcasting with Songs of Sorrow
The Gallifreyan Gentleman: Silent Wealth, Sonic Confidence, and the Doctor's Code of Living
Sugar Water Confidence
Dino Totems: Spirit Guides from Earth's First Gods
Pumpkin Sigils & Ritual Smoke
The Hózhó Compass
The Distortus Discipline – Order from Inner Mutation
Witchcraft for the Cold-Blooded Soul
Moonlight Over the Blessingway
Water, Interrupted: When the Body Forgets How to Hold On

Deformed but Divine: Embracing Your Asymmetry
Hexes in the Henhouse: The Farm Witch's Guide to Power
The Reversed Flame: A Grimoire of Inverted Power
Salt, Cells, and Sanity: Reclaiming Balance with Diabetes Insipidus
King of the Broken: Crowning the Flawed Self
Moonlight Scars: Emo Moon Magick and the Art of Lunar Sorrow
Noose Spells: Magick of the Hanging Rope
The Goth Cathedral: Rituals of the Broken and Beautiful
The Cretaceous Codex: Dino Spirits and Fossil Magick
The Turkey Bones Ritual
Nine Lives of Manifestation: Unlocking Bastet's Reality Codes
Chaos Muscles: Building Strength from Twisted Pain
Emo Blood Magick: The Veins of Power
The 3AM Flood: Nighttime Urination, Sleep Loss, and the DI Spiral
The Silence Between the Stars
The Lemon Method: Sour Your Way to Success
Starlit Sovereign
The Rite of Twelve Gates: Walking the Gates of the Duat.
Cornbread and Conjure: Recipes for Riches and Rootwork
The Black Rose Rituals: Emo Love Spells and Obsession Magick
The Eternal Goodbye: Death Magick and Rebirth Rituals
Sinkrot: The Drain That Remembers
The Hybrid Mindset: Thinking Beyond Evolution
Bone Dry: Navigating Dehydration Before It Breaks You
Wreathcraft: Winter Sigils and Yuletide Spells
The Rite of Twelve Mouths
S'mores of the Damned: Haunted Recipes for Halloween Night

Rethink the Drink: A Beverage Survival Guide for DI Warriors

The Shadow Chord: Guitar Magick and Sonic

Malformed Yet Majestic: Leading When You Feel Wrong Inside

The Cursed Diary: Ink-Stained Spells of the Emo Soul

Anxiety Off Switch: Emergency Reset for a Fried Nervous System

The Energy Heist: How to Take Back Your Life from Drainers

Beyond the Bathroom: Rebuilding Your Social Life With DI

Coyote's Gift for Decision Makers

Ghoul-Goo: Spooky S'mores You'll Die For

Echoes in the Mirror: Scrying and Self-Destruction Magick

Thread and Thorn: Stitching Spells from Rural Cloth

The Mogwai Mind: Building Untouchable Wealth from Small Ideas

Be Your Own Guide: Trust Your Inner Compass

Hormones in Chaos: The Endocrine Puzzle of Diabetes Insipidus

ChronoCleanse: Detox Your Biological Timeline

The Limb You Hide Is the One That Saves You

Leaves, Bones, and Whisper Spells

The Dinosaur Mindset: Prehistoric Tactics for Modern Wealth

Clawing Back Control: A Bastet Method for Boundaries and Empowerment

Samhain Codes of the Forgotten

Orange Alchemy: The Autumnal Spellbook

Monster Within, Master Without

The Sigil That Sleeps

Hearthcraft: Yule Hearth Sigils and Winter Warmth Spells

Temple of the Purring Moon: Rituals from Bastet's Lineage

When the Earth Remembers Your Footsteps

Food for Mood: Eat to Heal Depression, Not Just Survive It
Witch of the Kudzu Vine: Southern Pagan Wealth Secrets
The Invisible Diagnosis: Advocating for Yourself With DI
The Coffin's Lullaby: Sleep Magick and Nightmares as Portals
Ashes of the Will: Rituals for Erasing the Self
The Fracture Rite: Shattering the Magickal Core
Funeral Candles: The Art of Emo Flame Magick
The Black Grimoire: A Blank Ritual for Writing in Absence
Phantom Thirst: A Halloween Survival Guide for Diabetes Insipidus
The Hollow Crown: Emo Royalty and Magick of the Outcast King
Sandpainting for the Soul
Falling Into Balance: Using the Extra Hour to Recalibrate Life
100 Southern Superstitions That Still Work
The DI Child: A Parent's Guide to Raising Hydrated, Happy Kids
The Jungle of Shame: Escaping the Hidden Lab of Doubt
The Witch's Toast: S'mores Spells and Creepy Confections
The Hoodoo Pantry: Spells from the Mason Jar
The Immortal Fortune: Secret Wealth Lessons from Captain Jack Harkness
The Specter's Embrace: Magick for Channeling Ghostly Lovers
Grateful Waters: A Thanksgiving Survival Guide for Diabetes Insipidus
The Seizure Gospel
Harvestbind: Autumn Sigils and Samhain Spells
Doctor Who: The Algorithmic Awakening
Silent Nights, Steady Waters: A Christmas Survival Guide for Diabetes Insipidus
The Extra Hour Effect: How One Hour Can Transform Everything

Blade Between the Breaths

Running with the Mountain Shadows

Echoes of the Failed Experiment – Becoming a Living Legacy

Swamp Witches & River Ghosts: Real Southern Hauntings

Cornbread Prophecies: Magical Recipes from a Southern Table

Doctor Who: The Signal in the Star

Bloomcraft: Spring Sigils and Equinox Enchantments

Vanisher: How to Disappear from the Internet Without Losing Your Life

The Ultimate Christmas Cookie Cookbook

The Unbreakable Parent: How to Mentally Survive Raising Kids in a Broken World

Time Debt: How to Reclaim the Hours You Didn't Know You Lost

One Month, One Million: Unconventional Cash Creation Tactics

Doctor Who: The Cyber Conversion Protocol

Black Friday Frenzy: The Art of Finding Hidden Online Deals

The Grimoire Buried Under the Apple Tree

Digital Couponing Masterclass: Your Step-by-Step Guide to Black Friday Savings

The Fire Inside the Flint

Shadows on the Ceiling: The Emo Guide to Astral Magick

The Bone-Eaters Beneath Us

Black Friday Bundle Blueprint: Creating Irresistible Product Packages for Maximum Sales

Thirteen Nights of Unbinding

Doctor Who: Engines of Influence

Pumpkin Spice Alchemy: Recipes of Fire and Frost

When Raptor Met Rexy: Prehistoric Lessons in Wild Romance

Oblivion's Candle: Burn the Path Behind You

Campfire Curses and Chocolate: A Halloween S'mores Grimoire
The Wallet That Wasn't Mine: Breaking Free from Inherited Scarcity
The Cola Zodiac: What Your Fizz Says About Your Fate
Frostfire Fortune: Unlocking Winter's Hidden Prosperity
Signal Jamming: Detox Your Brain from Info Overload
The Dust of the Forgotten Rite
The Golden Cat Sigils: Drawing Power in Bastet's Name
Mud Magick: The Prosperity of Getting Dirty
Savory Spicefall: Beyond the Pumpkin Pie
Pumpkin Spice Apothecary Kitchen
The Pumpkin Spice Economy: Turning Trends into Billions
The Ember Veil: 13 Nights of Fire Magick
Financial Freeze: When Earning Triggers Panic
The Gingerbread Alchemist: Sweet Recipes with a Twist
Biosynth Power: Programming Yourself from Scratch
Echoes from the Talking Circle
Truffle Alchemy: Fungus of Fortune
Spores of Power: The Truffle Witch's Handbook
Doctor Who: The Tower That Speaks
The Mycelium Veil: Truffle Magick Unbound
Broke But Ashamed: Healing the Shame Wound of Debt
The Evergreen Mind: Growth Through Winter Stillness
The Black Veil Truffle Rite
The Voice Beneath Symbols
Witchlight on the Bayou: Swamp Spells for Sovereignty
I Grew Up Poor and Now I Sabotage My Success
The Lantern of Hollow Souls
Shutdown Survival: A Citizen's Guide to Thriving When Government Stops
When Abundance Feels Like a Threat: Healing the Hidden Fears of Enough

The Scarecrow Grimoire
Owls of the October Veil
Candlewax and Curses: A Halloween Spellbook
Excavating the Inner Fossil – Transforming Fossilized Thoughtforms into Tools of Power
The Yule Witch's Spellbook: Magick for the Holiday Season
Haunted Christmas: Ghost Stories for Winter Nights
The Christmas Survival Guide: Thriving Through the Chaos
The Bone Orchard Rites
Haunted Commerce: The Ghost in the Marketplace
When Money Triggers the Inner Child
Silent Night with the Silence: A Christmas Thriller
The Lightning Crown: Living and Leading Through Seizures
TARDIS Tidings: Festive Stories from the Whoniverse
Autumn Reset: Slowing Down Without Falling Behind
The Trillion Dollar Soul: Rewriting the Currency of Reality
Truffle Eclipse Magick
Micro-Manifestations: Quick Magick That Works
5-Minute Rituals for Busy Witches
The Marshmallow Massacre: Halloween Treats with a Sinister Twist
Blood and Blackberry Thorns
Magickal Mornings: Rituals for a Blessed Christmas Day
Embers of the All-Hallows Fire
The Pumpkin Market Collapse
The Hour You Gained: Transforming Time Into Power
The Chamber Must Be Sealed: Mastering the Power of Controlled Access
The Cursed Manuscript of Petosiris
The Festive Hearth: Creating Holiday Traditions
Darkness Rising: Thriving as Nights Grow Longer
Harvesting Time: Turning the Year's End Into Your New Beginning

Petosiris and the 13th Zodiac Key
Wagewound: When Paychecks Become Identity Prisons
Walls That Watch
The Silent Feast: Rituals of Power in the Longest Night
The Distortus Legacy : Becoming a Deformed King in a Perfect World
The Hollow Masks
The Gratitude Furnace: Forging Gold from Thanks
Feast of Inner Gold: Eating for Energy and Enlightenment
Haunted Commerce: The Season of Spending Spirits
Fear Bonds: How Panic Creates Profit
Black Friday E-Commerce Playbook: Sales Tactics to Skyrocket Your Holiday Revenue
Budgeting for Black Friday: A Holiday Savings Planner
Haunting the Harvest Moon
The Warrior's Water: Emergency Preparedness for People With DI
The First Sip of the Year: A New Year's Survival Guide for Diabetes Insipidus
Doctor Who: The Thirteenth Node
The Unseen Struggle: Mental Health, Anxiety, and Chronic Thirst
The Hearth's Hidden Ledger: Counting Energies as Currency
The Gift Alchemist: Turning Any Offering Into Gold
The Papyrus of the Bound Spirit
The Magick of Leftovers: Transmutation in the Fridge
Frost and Fortune: Christmas Wealthcraft for the Modern Magus
Last-Minute Gifts: Creative Ideas on a Budget
10 Secrets to Surviving Holiday Crowds
The Witch's Dow Jones
The Witches' Graveyard Shift
Pumpkin Sigils: Carving Rites for Midnight Power

The Secret Shopper's Black Friday Guide: How to Get Early Access and VIP Deals

Fever in the Foundation

The Neuralyzer Reset: Reprogram Your Morning Routine

Lightning Lessons of the White Painted Woman

The Enchanted Snowflake

The Magic Sip: Surviving Disney Parks with Diabetes Insipidus

The One Who Draws Through You

Santa's Secrets: A Magical Holiday Planner

Silent Bells, Loud Miracles: Self-Help for the Season of Stillness

The Sugar Spell Codex: Confectionary Magick of Christmas

Autumn Hexcraft: Fallen Leaves, Fallen Barriers

Sleep Like a Fortress: Build a Life Where Insomnia Can't Survive

Nowhere Was Ever Home

Christmas Under the Stars: A Celestial Holiday Guide

Rentproof: How to Never Be Evicted Again

Workless: Escape the 9-5 Without Being Broke

The Gilded Gift: A Wealth Altar for Christmas Morning

The Black Friday Grimoire

The Hollowing: Ceremonies of Spiritual Collapse

Doctor Who: The Nameless Signal

Where the Eagle Hides His Courage

The Dwarf Tyrant's Ascent: Claiming Power in a World of Giants

The Currency of the Dead: Trading with Spectral Bankers

The Icebound Witch: Survival and Magick in the Cold

The Emergency Money Mind: Constant Crisis, Zero Calm

Thirst & Roses: A Valentine's Survival Guide for Diabetes Insipidus

Springing Into Clarity: Mastering the Energy Shift of Daylight Saving

Speed of the Nanotyrant: Agile Strategies for Life's Hunt

The 90-Day Reset: A Science-Backed Guide to Reinvent Yourself Before the New Year

The Coil of Thorns

Timegates Unleashed

Dopamine Fasting 2.0: Rewiring Your Brain in a World of Overstimulation

The Nanotyrannus Mutation: Embracing Your Differentiated Form

Unwritten January: How to Use the Blank Page of the Year to Re-Author Your Life

Feast of the Forgotten Spirits: Ancestor Magick for the Holidays

The Burnout Codex: A System for Thriving Beyond Stress

I Don't Deserve to Have Money

When the King Doesn't See You: The Shadow Predator's Guide

The Reset Ritual :A Guide to Shedding Last Year's Weight—Emotional and Physical—by Spring Cleaning Your Soul

Calendar Alchemy: Learn to Bend Time and Productivity around Your Natural Rhythms

The Mirror Contract: A One-Sentence Agreement with Yourself that Unlocks Real Change

The Nile Formula: Sacred Flow for Millionaire Minds

Forward Momentum: Productivity Rituals for the Lost Hour

Harvest Gold: Wealth Magick of Pumpkin Spice Commerce

The Magick of Christmas Lights: Illuminating Holiday Rituals

Cranberry Crown: Royal Self-Worth through Ritual Meals

Petosiris and the Worms of the Feathered Throne

The Evergreen Equation: Self-Help for Sustained Growth

The Rain Will Wash Us Away: Emo Weather Magick
Snowlight Shadows: Magick Under Frozen Stars
Doctor Who: Merger of Empires
The Light Within the Feast: Magickal Wealth of Yuletide Flame
Momentum Machines: Small Habits Designed to Snowball into Unstoppable Forward Motion
Calm Spells: Magickal Solutions for Anxiety Relief
Santa's Final List: The Naughty Never Leave
The Mystic's Guide to Banishing Worry
The Silence Dividend: Turning Quiet Mornings into Compounding Growth All Year
Charmed Stillness: Rituals to Ease the Mind
Blood Spiral Ascension
The Vanishing Heart Invocation
Crystal Calm: Harnessing Stones for Anxiety
The Nano Tyrant Code: Strength in the Small Predator
The Energy Ledger: Accounting Methods for Vitality, Not Just Money
Snowglobe Mindset: Shake Up Your Thoughts, Settle Into Peace
The Weight of the Feather: Anubis's Codes for Soul Balance
Pocket Peppermint Power: Tiny Rituals for Big Holiday Energy
Shadowkeeper of the Golden Jackal: Anubis's Path to Energetic Protection
The Witch's Breath: Anxiety Relief Through Magickal Breathing
The Tiny Ember: Pocket Motivation for Cold Days
Stocking Sorcery: Mini Spells for Holiday Luck and Prosperity
Warm Hands, Steady Heart: Micro Grounding for Winter Anxiety

The Fourteenth Doctor: A New Beginning (David Tennant, 2022–2023)

The Fifteenth Doctor: Rewriting the Stars
(Ncuti Gatwa, 2023–2025)

Santa's Shortcut to Success: Micro Habits for a Better New Year

The Midnight Cocoa Manifesto: Comfort Rituals for Hard Nights

Why I Can't Save: Trauma Blocks to Financial Planning

Dino Brain, Mega Goals: Rewire Yourself for Savage Success.

Jurassic Profit: Unearth Your Inner Millionaire Fossil

Scales & Softness: Dating with Dino Heart

Carnotaurus Dreams.

Red Willow Thinking.

Reindeer Resilience: How to Keep Going When You're Exhausted

Candlewick Courage: Lighting Strength in Dark Seasons.

Elf-Mode Focus: Fast Attention Fixes for Busy Seasons

Futureproof Feelings: Emotional Skill-Building for Resilience No Matter What the New Year Brings

The 90-Day Rewire: Transform Your Neural Pathways Before Spring Blooms

Jolly Rich: Christmas Micro-Money Magick for Fast Prosperity.

Gingerbread Gratitude: Mini Practices for a Happier Holiday

Trauma-Spending: When Money Becomes a Drug

Goal Skeletons: Build Minimalist Frameworks for Resolutions That Last

The Snarl Strategy: Growling Back at a World That Silenced You

The Hourglass Reset: Reclaiming What the Clock Took

Yule Claw: Dino Rites of Light in the Darkness

Sacred Circles: Grounding Rituals for Anxious Souls

Clockstopper's Gut: Rebuilding the Core of Time

Winterfire Drive: Harness the Cold Season's Stillness to Ignite Deep Motivation

The 5-Minute Productivity Hack: Small Steps to Big Results

Light Ascending: A Self-Help Guide to Longer Days

Inner Economy: Trade Self-Doubt for Confidence Like a High-Value Currency

Simple Success: Decluttering Your Life for Better Results

The Resilient Mind: Thriving in Tough Times

The 2026 Playbook: Mastering the Year Ahead

The Spring Sleep Solution: Conquering Fatigue After Time Change.

The Hormonal Compass: Navigate Back to Your Youth

Golden Vision: Eating for Your Eye Color with the Power of Ghee

Lionhearted Love: Strength in Relationships

MiB Mindset: Think Like a Cosmic Agent

The Ladder of Small Wins: Climb Out of Stagnation by Stacking Micro-Victories

The Momentum Hour: Gaining More in Less Time.

The Year of You: A Self-Help Blueprint for Unapologetic Self-Ownership

The Dust That Watches You Back.

The Astral Parent

Shadow of the King: The Nanotyrannus Parable

Tiny Tidings of Triumph: Small Wins That Change Your Life

Dwarf Tyrant Rising: When You're the One They Overlook

The Bank Account Mirror: Healing How You See Yourself Through Money

Cretaceous Black

When Love Costs Too Much: Romantic Triggers and Financial Wounds

Dream-Eater's Guide to Wealth

Unzipped Reality: The Jacket That Opens Portals

The Power of No: How to Set Boundaries and Get Rich

Keeper of the Desert Veil: Anubis's Teachings on Illusion & Truth

Redacted Stargates: Stories the SGC Buried

The Clock That Dripped Time

Doctor Who: The Silent Acquisition

Hairline Manifestation: Unlocking Power at the Edge of Thought

Cash-Eater Crickets: How Insects Predict Economic Collapse

Dead Pet Whisperer: Grief Alchemy from the Other Side

The Love Algorithm Is Broken: Hack Romance Before It Hacks You

The Rite of the 8-Limbed Seal

Melt the Moon: A Fire Ritual to Reshape Emotion

Venomous Miracles: Healing Through the Poison Path

Wealth Without Water: The Post-Aquatic Rich Life

The Butterfly Betrayal: When Change Turns on You

The Quiet Upgrade: How Humans Are Secretly Rebuilding Themselves Without Asking Permission

Nobody Taught Us This: The Missing Human Manual for Money, Energy, and Self-Respect

You Were Never Broken: Why Most People Are Reacting Normally to an Unstable World

After the Noise Ends: How Humans Reset When the World Finally Goes Quiet

The Month That Tells the Truth: Why January Reveals What the Rest of the Year Hides

Tremors Party Unleashed: The Ultimate Guide to a Graboids Birthday Bash

Cold Start Human: Rebooting Motivation Without Forcing Momentum

The Year that doesn't start until they say

Love Without Performance: What Connection Looks Like When No One Is Watching

February Is a Mirror: What Love Exposes About You

How We Learned Love Wrong: Uninstalling Cultural Myths About Connection

You Are Not Too Much: Why Needing Love Is Not a Flaw

The Crooked Fence Covenant: Backwoods Boundaries and Witch Wealth

The Day That Keeps Repeating: Why Your Life Feels Stuck—and How to Shift It Gently

Nothing Changes Until Something Softens: Escaping Repetition Without Violence to Yourself

Same Life, Different Ending: How Tiny Choices Rewrite Repetition

The Loop Isn't Punishment: Why You're Being Asked to Learn, Not Suffer

Panic at the Register: Retail Anxiety and Public Shame

The Secret Formula to Becoming an Influencer in 90 Days

The New Rich: How to Retire by 35

Digital Nomad Secrets: How to Travel the World and Make Millions

Burn Your Waiting Room: Escape the Delay Spiral

Strapped for Pleasure: A Complete Guide to Pegging and Strap-On Play

Locked in Desire: A Guide to Chastity Play and Intimate Control

Burrowing into History: Groundhog Day Through the Ages

The Shadow Forecast: The Science of Groundhog Day

Choice Cascades: How One Decision in January Sets Ripples for the Whole Year

The Anti-Anxiety Blueprint: Mastering Fear and Stress for Success

The Ancestral Path of the Jackal Priest

Winterborn Titans: Giants of Ice and Stone
The Extinction Spire
The Emotion That Made Me Millions
Delete Their Voice: Become Unreachable
The Frostbound Mysteries: Mythical Beings of January's Chill
The Roar Within: Unlocking Your Potential
From Burrow to Sky: Groundhog Day Explained
The Boogey Book: Festive Ward-Off Edition
Fooled Ya! The Psychology Behind Great Pranks
April Fools' Alchemy: Transforming Everyday Items into Pranks
Anchor Habits: Root Yourself in Unshakable Routines That Endure Seasonal Change
Emerald Waters: A St. Patrick's Day Survival Guide for Diabetes Insipidus
The Groundhog's Legacy: Myths, Legends, and Facts
Six Weeks of Mystery: The Truth Behind Groundhog Day
The Upgrade Mind: Tech-Like Patches and Updates for Your Mental Operating System
Moon Blood, Star Flesh: Embracing Your Hybrid Nature
Groundhog Lore and Legend: A Complete Guide
You Are the Lie They Can't Kill
Download a Different Reality
The Quiet Advantage: Winning Without Announcing Yourself
A Year of Gratitude: Unlocking Joy
Touch Grass: A Pagan Reset for a Burned-Out Digital World
Cold Start Wealth: Building Financial Power from a Standing Still Point
Astrology Without Fate: Using Cycles Without Surrendering Control
The Future is Remote: Work Less, Earn More, Live Anywhere
Harvest of Silence

The Algorithm Knows Your Name

April Fools' Day for Introverts

Soft Power Systems: Influence That Doesn't Exhaust You

Practical Magick for Real Life: Focus, Intent, and Follow-Through

January Is a Lie: Designing Momentum Without the Calendar

Universal Flow: Managing DI in High-Energy Theme Parks

Electric Allure: Exploring Erotic Electro-Play

The Masked Embrace: Exploring Sensory Deprivation

The Ultimate April Fools' Survival Guide

Splashproof Survival: Waterparks & Wave Pools with DI

Agile Predator, Still King: Crafting Your Speed in a World That Celebrates Size

The Shadow Feast: Groundhog Day's Sinister Side

The Bug's Business Model

Edge of Bliss: Mastering the Art of Tease and Denial

Midnight Alchemy: Rituals for Transformation Between the Old Year and the New

Punxsutawney Bloodlines: A Groundhog Day Horror

The Burrower: Groundhog Day's Darkest Secrets

Buried Alive: A Groundhog Day Horror Story

Blood Moon Markets: The Witch's Guide to Wealth Magick

The Groundhog's Shadow: What It Means for the World

Seasonal Shadows: The Groundhog Day Phenomenon

The Shadow's Curse: A Groundhog Day Horror Tale

Punxsutawney Revealed: A Guide to Groundhog Day

Safari Hydration: Zoo & Wildlife Park Survival for DI

The Foolproof Prank Planner

Latex Lust: Embracing Fetish Fashion **is a sophisticated**

Whip & Whisper: The Dynamics of Impact Play

The Shadow Burrow Chronicles: Horror Beneath the Ground

Frozen Shadows: A Groundhog Day Thriller

The Groundhog's Revenge: A February Nightmare

Burrow of the Damned
Everyday Enchantment: Magickal Practices for Modern Living
Budget Bliss: The Easy Path to Financial Freedom
Six More Weeks of Terror
The Oxygen Debt
The Ice Veil: Mystical Beasts of January's Shadows
Roots That Remember
Polar Myths: Creatures of the Icy Abyss
The Marginalia Covenant
AI and the Occult: Digital Spirits, Sigils, and Cyber-Witchcraft
Roleplay Realms: Crafting Fantasies and Scenes
The Last Clean River
Lover in the Shadows: A Groundhog Day Tale
Buried Hearts: A Groundhog Day Gothic Romance
Anubis Wept for Petosiris
The Lantern Knows Your Name
Rituals of the Last Shadow
The Bell That Rings for No One
Shadows of Love and Death
The Groundhog's Bride: A Dark Valentine's Tale
Frozen Kisses: A Horror Romance for Groundhog Day
The Creative Spark: Igniting Your Passion Projects
From Cub to King: A Journey of Transformation
Six Weeks to Midnight: A Groundhog Day Romance
Tide of the Unclean
Burrow of Desire: A Groundhog Day Paranormal Romance
The Shadow Magick Almanac: Harnessing Groundhog Day Energies
AI for Emo Influencers: Growing an Online Following Without the Anxiety
AI for the Melancholy Millionaire: Making Money Without Social Interaction

Winter's Grip: A Horror Romance Beneath the Frost
Shadowed Hearts: A Love Buried in Winter's Chill
The Shadow Lover: A Groundhog Day Gothic Love Story
Beneath the Burrow: A Groundhog Day Thriller
The Punxsutawney Conspiracy
The Crimson Pact: Emo Blood Oath Magick
The Shadows of Gallifrey: A Doctor Who Horror Collection
Whispers in the Vortex: Chilling Tales from the TARDIS
AI Ghostwriting for Emo Souls: How to Make Money Writing Without Trying
The Anti-Social Emo's Guide to AI-Powered Freelancing
Emo AI Therapy: Talking to Robots When Humans Suck
Cry & Collect: AI-Powered Passive Income for Emos
The Weeping Angel Chronicles: A Collection of Terror
Dating Without the Mask
The Clockwork Menace: Horror Stories from the Future
Tender Doesn't Mean Weak
Not a Burden, Not a Bonus
Dalek Nightmares: Stories of Ultimate Extermination
The Empty Child's Curse: Tales of Horror and Fear
The TARDIS Ghost Files: Hauntings Across the Universe
Soft Armor, Open Heart
Chosen Gently
Love That Doesn't Rush You
Financial Gaslighting: When You're Made to Feel Crazy About Money.
After the Bees Went Silent
The Soil Knows Your Name
The Quantum Magick Codex: Unlocking the Hidden Laws of Reality
The Gingerbread Golem's Awakening: A Tale of Sweet Revenge

The Gingerbread Golem Chronicles: Guardians of Frost Hollow

The Power of Focus: Eliminate Distractions, Achieve Greatness

Sacred Submission: The Dynamics of D/s Relationships

The Magick of Numbers: Unlocking the Hidden Codes of the Universe

Blood and Bones: The Ancient Magick of Life and Death

Doctor Who: The Collapse Dividend

Thesis of the Unremembered

Desired as You Are

The Energy Budget of Love

Romancing Your Potential: The Love Month Growth Guide

Seen, Not Studied

Screams from the Void: Horror Stories Inspired by Doctor Who

The Silence Is Watching: A Collection of Dread

Under the Floorboards

The House of Feathers and Fangs

Emperor Bones, Hollow Crown

Goreglyphs of the Boiling Deep

The Coven That Screamed Back

The Stacks That Breathe

Love That Adapts

Nightmares on Gallifrey: Frights from the Doctor Who Universe

Apache Ways to Heal Powerfully

Belos Left No Corpses

The Algorithm Hates You (Good.)

Starve the Soul, Feed the Flame

Romance Without Apology

The Carbon Illusion

Your Nervous System is Your GPS

Where Rest Learns Your Name: Six Gentle Bedtime Stories for Minds That Work Differently

Soft Armor for Tender Nights: Six 5-Minute Bedtime Stories for Hearts That Have Been Hurt

Paws of Night, Path of Stars: Six 5-Minute Bedtime Stories Guided by Bastet and Anubis

When the Mind Needs a Lamp: Six 5-Minute Bedtime Stories for Gentle Mental Health Care

Imbolc Roar: Awakening the Dino Flame

The Titan Never Died

Witchflesh Harvest

Become the Thought They Can't Unsee

Golden Threads: The Sensuality of Body Worship

Chains of Desire: Exploring the Beauty of Restraint

Glyphs Written in Organs

Living Below the Line

Palismen Don't Scream—Until They Do

The Boiling Isles Devour the Weak

Hexside Anatomy Lab

Philip Wittebane and the First Body

Money PTSD: When Trauma Hijacks Your Finances

Brother, Bone, and Betrayal

Lipstick Like a Weapon: A Goth Girl's Guide to Emotional Dominance, Boundaries, and Quiet Intimidation

The Scar Is the Portal

Don't Grow—Mutate

Built from Breakdown: The Collapse Code

The Collector's First Lesson

Glyph Failure Syndrome

Philip Wittebane and the Discipline of Lies

The Making of Belos

Flesh Does Not Belong

The Golden Guard Prototypes

Coven Marks as Control Wounds
The Voice Belos Invented
The Boogeyman Within: Shadow Work for Personal Transformation
The Energy Edge: Reclaiming Your Power
Mindful March: A Quick Guide to Intentional Living
Love on Autopilot: Rekindle Your Relationship Instantly
Spring Renewal: Refresh Your Mindset Before the Equinox
Velvet Control: The Subtle Art of Erotic Choking
Erotic Shadows: Playing with Voyeurism and Exhibitionism
The Green Pulse Awakens
Equinox Bones
Immortality Is a Disease
Cold-Blooded Focus
The Invasive Advantage
The Lonely Assassin's Love: A Weeping Angel Romance
Philip Is Still Inside
Become the Signal That Replaces the Noise
When the Soil Says Yes
Shedding What No Longer Protects You

www.ingramcontent.com/pod-product-compliance
Lightning Source LLC
LaVergne TN
LVHW022220200926
848481LV00006B/2045
9798295615818